THE TRANSITION FROM SCHOOL TO WORK

The Transition from School to Work

Michael West & Peggy Newton

CROOM HELM
London & Canberra

NICHOLS PUBLISHING COMPANY
New York

© 1983 Michael West and Peggy Newton
Croom Helm Ltd, Provident House, Burrell Row,
Beckenham, Kent BR3 1AT

British Library Cataloguing in Publication Data

West, Michael
　The transition from school to work.
　1. High school graduates – Employment –
　Great Britain
　I. Title　　II. Newton, Peggy
　306'36　　HD6276.G7
　ISBN 0-7099-2758-4

First published in the United States of America 1982
by Nichols Publishing Company, Post Office Box 96, New York,
NY 10024

Library of Congress Cataloging in Publication Data

West, Michael A.
　The transition from school to work.

　Bibliography: p.
　Includes index.
　1. High school graduates – Employment – United
States. 2. Youth – Employment – United States.
3. Vocational guidance – United States.
4. United States – Occupations. I. Newton,
Peggy. II. Title.
HD6273.W43 1982　306'.36'088055　82-10611
ISBN 0-89397-140-5

Printed and bound in Great Britain

CONTENTS

List of Tables and Figures	vii
Preface	xi
1. Introduction and Background to the Study	1
2. Attitudes to Teachers and Schools	21
3. Occupational Choice	42
4. Finding Jobs and Sources of Help	57
5. Aims and Attainments	77
6. Entry into Work	94
7. Attitudes to Work	114
8. Attitudes to Supervisors	134
9. Job Changing	144
10. The Transition	159
11. Conclusions	173
Appendices	190
Bibliography	208
Index	216

TABLES AND FIGURES

Percentages of pupils choosing items to describe teachers' professional and personal characteristics 25
Percentages of respondents choosing items to describe teachers in the two schools .. 27
Percentages in the 'A' and 'B' bands of Woodbank school choosing items to describe teachers 27
The relationship between descriptions of teachers and educational ability 27
Percentages of girls and boys choosing items to describe teachers 30
Attitudes to leaving school held by boys and girls 30
Percentages of favourable and unfavourable items chosen by pupils in their descriptions of schools 33
Percentages of pupils in Woodbank and Brookvale schools choosing items to describe their schools 33
Attitudes of males and females to working life compared with school life 36
Occupational choices of respondents 47
Reasons given by school-leavers for their occupational choices 47
Number of school-leavers from Woodbank and Brookvale schools choosing occupations of socio-economic Status 1 to socio-economic Status 5 48
Length of time taken by all respondents and by 'A' band and 'B' band pupils to secure their first jobs 60
Number of job applications made by school-leavers before they were given their first jobs 60
Responses to the question: 'Why do you think

vii

you were given the job?'	65
Responses to the question: 'How did you hear about your job?'	65
Responses to the question: 'Did you get any help from the school or the Careers Advisory Service in finding this job?'	65
Retrospective assessment of help from the Careers Advisory Service in finding jobs- 2½ years into working life	68
Helpfulness of school in giving information about different jobs - six months before leaving school	68
Retrospective assessment of help from school in finding jobs - 2½ years into working life	68
Occupational aims and attainments	81
Correspondence between jobs aimed at and jobs attained	83
Status of jobs aimed at and obtained by pupils from Woodbank and Brookvale schools	83
School-leavers' attitudes to their having to take jobs which were different from those at which they originally aimed	90
School-leavers' reasons for accepting the jobs they were doing	90
Length of time for which school-leavers were willing to train for a job	101
Type of training received by young people entering work	101
Attitudes of young workers to the idea of attending day or evening classes	104
Time spent introducing young workers to the work and the firm	106
Socialization to working life: three stage process	112
School-leavers' attitudes to work at nine months and thirty months into their working lives	118
Distribution of workplaces of jobs of respondents	123
Job interest attributed by respondents to their jobs	123
Type of wage paid to young workers	130
Weekly wage of young workers	130
Percentages of school-leavers considering changing their jobs, and percentages feeling settled in their jobs	131
Percentages of school-leavers interested in promotion or in changing jobs at their places of work	131
Young workers' descriptions of their	

relations with co-workers and supervisors	136
Number of job changes made by young workers at 9 months and 30 months after leaving school	154
Reasons given by young workers for their changes in employment	154
The relationship between job changing and degree of correspondence between occupational aims and attainments	156
Differences in perceptions of changes in home life between males and females	163
Average agreement with alienation statements: males, females, 'A' band and 'B' band workers	163
The importance of different factors in choice of jobs	170

PREFACE

The study reported in this book examines a crucial phase in development for many adolescents and was conducted between 1976 and 1979. Since the beginning of the study economic circumstances have changed in Britain with increasing unemployment and more limited opportunities for young people. The results of our study which relate to the occupational attainments of school leavers, are almost certainly not a reflection of the current situation. The prospect facing school leavers is now even more limited and the learning to be derived from the study therefore carries with it even greater potential for useful application in understanding and alleviating the stresses experienced by young people during this period.
We would like to record our gratitude to the young people who so willingly and co-operatively gave of their time to provide the answers to the many questions with which we plied them.
We are also grateful to all the interviewers who worked so hard to produce the information which forms the kernel of this book. A number of people were involved in the study at different stages but Jean Fish has helped to carry it through from its beginnings to its completion by her tact in making and maintaining initial contacts with the schools, employers and the adolescents, and her enthusiasm at all stages of the study.
The study described in this book was supported by a Social Science Research Council Programme Grant to Professor Geoffrey Stephenson for work on "The Social Psychology of Organizations'.
Professor Stephenson has been a constant source of advice, support and encouragement and we are very grateful for all his help. Many members of the Social Psychology Research Unit at the University

of Kent at Canterbury have made useful comments on the book and in particular, Kevin Durkin suggested improvements to Chapter 9. We would also like to thank Parvin Akhtar for checking and rechecking the manuscript. Finally, Kay Evans has influenced the presentation and writing throughout, and her hard work, advice and constant encouragement merit the greatest thanks.

Chapter One

INTRODUCTION AND BACKGROUND TO THE STUDY

> 'Your clothes will be looked after for you, too', said Mr. Murdstone, 'as you will not be able, yet awhile, to get them for yourself. So you are now going off to London, David, with Mr. Quinion, to begin the world on your own account.'
> 'In short, you are provided for', observed his sister, 'and will please do your duty.'
> Though I quite understood that the purpose of this announcement was to get rid of me, I have no distinct remembrance whether it pleased or frightened me. My impression is, that I was in a state of confusion about it, and, oscillating between the two points, touched neither.
> David Copperfield

It would not be surprising if many school-leavers experience a state of confusion during their transition from school to work, since within a relatively short period of time adolescents are expected to discard the role of dependent school child and assume the role of independent working adult. The consequent complex and profound changes which occur in their lives undoubtedly cause many to oscillate between feelings of anxiety and pleasure. During this period, the individual is required to choose an occupation, to find and apply for jobs, to learn the norms and values of the new world of work, to learn the intricacies of a new job and to become successfully integrated in a new organization. Influencing the performance of these tasks is a wide variety of social forces shaping the adolescent's expectations, attitudes and experiences. Schools, parents, peers, the media, careers teachers, national and local economic factors and past experience are among these forces, and an understanding of how these social agents and the individual interact, and how attitudes and experiences are shaped during the transition period, necessarily precedes informed attempts to ease the passage of the school child into the new role of working adult.

Despite the potential applications deriving from an understanding of this area, there is general acknowledgement of a paucity of reliable and informative research studies. Whilst individual aspects of the transition phase have received careful attention, relatively few studies have been carried out in which the transition period as a whole was considered. Of these few, some have concentrated on individual descriptions or case studies with a consequent neglect of revelations about overall trends, while the remainder have been somewhat rigidly tied to the reporting of statistical data to the exclusion of the rich, illustrative material which the reports of school leavers themselves can provide. We would argue that there is a need to integrate these approaches, using adolescents' own reports to provide supplementary information as an aid to the understanding of numerical results - and especially in an area as complex as this.

The study reported here represents an attempt to investigate a range of aspects of the transition from school to work, by examining adolescents' experiences and attitudes at selected points in the transition period. An attempt was made to achieve a balance between subjective descriptions and reports provided by the school leavers themselves, and statistical data   (For those interested in the results of statistical significance testing which was carried out on the data, full details are included in the appendices. Within the text the following conventions will be used: $p < 0.05$ will be described as 'significant'; $p < 0.01$ will be described as 'highly significant'). The precise details of the study cannot be understood however in isolation from the existing theoretical and research literature related to the period of transition from school to work. The topic which has received by far the most attention within this broad area is that of occupational choice.

OCCUPATIONAL CHOICE: THEORY AND RESEARCH

Ginzberg's Developmental Theory
Ginzberg et al (1951) were the first to attempt to devise a comprehensive theory of how individuals choose to enter particular occupations. They

conceptualised occupational choice as a sequence of developmental stages leading to entry into an occupation. The theory proposed three major stages: fantasy, tentative and realistic choices. The fantasy stage, according to the theory, occurs in early childhood when the child believes he or she can become anything that is attractive, and these fantasies are expressed in games of fire-fighting, space pilot, cops and robbers, shopkeeping, or whatever. The games are influenced by recent experiences, family, peers or television, and the preference a child expresses at this stage will have no regard for the skill or qualifications necessary. The important feature of the period is the lack of regard for the detailed consequences of choices. The child is likely to centre his or her attention upon the pleasant, beneficial or exciting features of the job, rather than upon sophisticated considerations such as security, pay, conditions or prospects.

The second period of tentative choices is subdivided into four stages: (1) interest; (2) capacity; (3) values and (4) transition. This period coincides roughly with the period of adolescence from eleven to seventeen years of age and the period is thought to be characterised by a growing awareness of the need for criteria by which reasoned choices can be made. The interest stage is the time when the individual begins to decide that some activities, pursuits and ideas are of more interest than others; the capacity stage represents the period during which the individual is directing attention at his or her own capabilities and turning thoughts about careers in those directions; the value stage involves the differentiation of those things that have intrinsic value e.g. personal satisfaction offered by a job, job prospects, income, artistic or scientific orientation; the transition stage involves the integration of all the information which the individual has derived during development through the tentative period, with the reality of the world of work.

The period of realistic choices during early adulthood is the final period in Ginzberg's developmental theory. It includes the stages of exploration , crystallisation and specification. With the limitations and information derived from the tentative period, the individual proceeds to realistically explore occupations that meet her or his requirements. The stage of crystallisation occurs when the individual feels there is sufficient information available for a firm decision about a career. Having crystallised his or her views, the individual then selects a specific occupation which calls for the requirements identified in the tentative stage. A recent restatement of Ginzberg's theory (Ginzberg, 1972) has resulted in a number of changes to the original formulation. Firstly, the idea of the decision-making process as being limited in duration has been abandoned in favour of a more open-ended interpretation so that, for example, the specification or crystallisation stages are now thought to be possible at any time. Previously, Ginzberg had limited decision-making to the ages between ten and twenty-one. Secondly, the decision-making process is now conceptualised as reversible. And thirdly, the previously held position that compromise between individuals' preferences and the constraints of the world of work was an essential part of occupational choice, has been abandoned in favour of the idea of 'optimisation'. Optimisation is described as the best occupational fit between individuals' desires and their changing circumstances.

Ginzberg's approach has been criticised (Roberts, 1975) because the subjects of the initial research upon which the theory was based were white, middle class and educationally successful. They were chosen because 'external environment interfered as little as possible with their freedom to pursue any occupation'. This has led to suggestions that the theory is only applicable (if it is applicable at all) to élite groups in the higher socio-economic strata of society.

Super's Theory
One of the most influential theorists in the field of occupational choice is Donald Super, whose formulations have drawn heavily upon the work of Ginzberg, upon the life stages concepts employed by Buehler (1933) and upon the idea of life stage tasks requiring completion which has been developed by Havighurst (1953). Super regarded the whole of life as comprising five major stages of (1) growth, 0 - 15 years of age; (2) exploration, 15 - 25 years; (3) establishment, 25 - 45 years; (4) maintenance, 45 - 65 years and (5) decline of occupational choice, 65 years and over. The theory incorporates twelve major propositions which have been well summarised by Child (1973) as follows:

(a) Individual differences should be considered (as important factors in occupational choice) such as abilities, interests and personality.
(b) 'Multipotentiality' exists in all of us, whereby the attributes mentioned in (a) above qualify us for a number of occupations by which we can succeed and gain satisfaction. These can be discerned using occupational interest inventories.
(c) Occupational ability patterns are present in us all. A characteristic pattern of abilities, interests and personality is more appropriate for some occupations than others.
(d) Vocational preference and competence change with time and experience, thus making choice and adjustment a continuous process.
(e) This process can be expressed as a series of life stages: growth, exploration, establishment, maintenance and decline.
(f) A career pattern (this is the level, sequence, frequency and duration of trial and stable jobs) is determined by external factors such as socio-economic background, work opportunities, and internal factors such as mental abilities, achievements and personality.
(g) Progress through life stages can be guided by counselling, in which self-knowledge of abilities and interests, aptitudes and career prospects are encouraged.
(h) The process of vocational development is essentially that of developing and implementing a self-concept; it is a compromise process in which the self-concept is a product of the interaction of inherited aptitudes, neural and endocrine make-up, opportunity to play various roles and evaluations of the extent to which the results of role-playing meet with the approval of superiors and fellows.
(i) The role-playing suggested in (h) above is a process of compromise between one's self-concept and the realities of external social factors.
(j) Work is a way of life. Adequate vocational and personal adjustment are most likely when both the nature of the work and the way of life that goes with it are congenial to the aptitudes, interests and values of

an individual.

Super maintains that the self-concept has a crucial influence in the process of occupational choice and his emphasis upon a developmental approach to theorising in this area has proved widely attractive to professionals in the careers guidance field (Super, 1957; Super et al, 1963; Super and Overstreet, 1968).

Holland's Theory
Holland (1966) sees people as developing occupational choices out of a search for work situations which provide outlets for their particular life-style. This life-style is compounded from values, interests, aptitudes, personality factors, intelligence and self-concepts. The life-style of the individual will orient him or her towards one of six occupational environments:

Realistic	e.g. labourer, farmer, truck-driver
Investigative	e.g. physicist, chemist, biologist
Social	e.g. teacher, social worker, missionary
Conventional	e.g. cashier, post-office clerk, secretary
Enterprising	e.g. politician, salesperson, publicity officer
Artistic	e.g. musician, writer, photographer

Jobs do not fall exclusively into these categories, nor are individuals seen to take up only one of the orientations. Individuals are thought to differ according to the arrangement of the hierarchy of their preferred orientations, and Holland sees choice as a matching process between personal hierarchies and the demands and satisfactions of particular jobs. Holland indicated that consistent and congruent pairing of the individual and the occupational environment is likely to result in stable vocational choice, higher vocational achievement, greater personal stability and greater satisfaction. The theory has been criticised, however, for its simplistic approach to what are very complex processes and for claiming theoretical status for what is only a series of hypotheses based on descriptive stereotypes.

Roe's Theory

Anne Roe has explored the relationship between personality and occupational choice, drawing upon the hierarchical need theory of Maslow (1954) and upon psychoanalytic interpretations of the importance of early childhood experiences (Roe and Siegelmann, 1964). Roe used information derived from biographical interviews and projective tests (e.g. Rorschach Ink Blot Test) to differentiate between life scientists, physical scientists and social scientists. This led her to suggest that personality differences exist between different occupational groups and that such differences are rooted in childhood. She drew upon Maslow's theory and the role of need arousal and satisfaction in personality development to stress the contributions of early parent-child relationships to later adult behaviour and occupational choice. Roe postulated six types of parent-child relationship (over-protective, over-demanding, rejecting, neglecting, casual and loving) and suggested these relationships predisposed people to particular occupational choices.

Roe's theory suffers from a number of drawbacks. Firstly, recent research has shown that early experience may not be as important as she suggests in determining adult behaviour (see, for example, Clarke and Clarke, 1976; Rutter, 1976). Secondly, the criticism levelled at Ginzberg's work applies to Roe's work too. The experimental basis of her theorising reveals an important bias since her subjects were drawn from occupations predominantly in the highest socio-economic status category. Her work has also been criticised as naive in attempting to account for the complexities of occupational choice with the use of just one factor (parent-child relationships).

Roberts' Theory

Within the last twenty years, in both the United States and Britain, the developmental theory of occupational choice expounded by Super has come to be widely accepted by practitioners in the careers guidance field and has influenced practice to a considerable extent (Hayes and Hopson, 1971; Jackson, 1973). Kenneth Roberts has challenged the theory on the grounds that it is of questionable validity and that basing practice upon the premises of the theory is likely as a result to have unwelcome consequences (Roberts, 1975).

He argues that the theory's main mistake lies

in treating individuals' occupational choices as central to the course of vocational development. According to Roberts, individuals rarely choose jobs - they simply take what is available. Consequently, in order to predict the type of job an individual will enter, it is more important to know about local job opportunities and the individual's educational qualifications than it is to know about his or her occupational aims. Secondly, Roberts argues, the career of the typical industrial worker cannot be regarded as an opportunity for self-actualisation and the implementing of a self-concept. Most workers are seen as accommodating to whatever jobs are available by adapting to the often unpleasant realities of the world of work. The developmental approach to careers guidance would (according to this argument) exacerbate rather than overcome the difficulties faced by school leavers seeking to enter the world of work, by raising their hopes and expectations to a level which cannot be matched in the real world.

Roberts proposes an alternative theory of occupational choice based on a key concept of 'opportunity structure'. Careers, in this alternative theory, are seen as developing in ways dictated by the opportunity structure to which individuals are exposed - first in education and then in employment. The ambitions of the individual are seen as reflecting the influence of the educational and employment structures through which he or she passes. This argument is based upon a number of sources of evidence. Firstly, the level at which school leavers enter the occupational hierarchy is determined primarily by their educational qualifications. Then, having entered a particular work organisation, individuals climb career 'ladders' only when they have entered an occupation in which such ladders are available. Secondly, the aspirations of school children are moulded by schools themselves - regardless of ability secondary modern school children will have lower aspirations than grammar school pupils. Thus, the argument goes 'in subtle but unmistakeable ways, distinct "climates of expectation" become associated with particular educational institutions and are internalised by their pupils'. Finally, upon entering occupations, individuals are further socialised to accept the particular world they have entered. Thus, in rewarding occupations, socialisation normally involves acquiring a professional identity (e.g. doctors, engineers, accountants) while in   less satisfying types of employment, the culture of the workplace may socialise the individual into acceptance of the unpleasant conditions of work whilst learning to enjoy 'secondary gratifications' such as the company of work-mates. On the basis of his arguments, Roberts proposes that careers guidance should be a matter of adjusting the individual to the opportunity structures to which he or she will have access; of helping individuals to solve the practical problems encountered in the transition from school to work; of serving the occupational system and of adjusting individuals to limited job opportunities, many of which allow little scope for personal development. These propositions have understandably generated considerable controversy (Daws, 1977), but until recently relatively little research has been carried out to assess the validity of Roberts' approach.

RESEARCH

A basic problem underlying all attempts to evaluate the relevance of different theories to practice, and the effectiveness of careers guidance has been the difficulty of identifying adequate criteria. Cherry (1974) chose the length of time the individual stayed in his or her first job as a criterion of success of vocational guidance. But, as Ashton and Field (1976) have pointed out, job changing can represent rational and constructive decision-making, and in many occupations frequent job changes can be a determinant of vocational success (e.g. construction and tourist industries). Watts and Kidd (1978) in a review of British research have argued that the choice of particular criteria is likely to reflect different value assumptions and different guidance aims, and must therefore be carefully examined.
Even given these problems, Watts and Kidd were still able to conclude that some forms of guidance are more effective than others in their impact upon satisfaction of clients entering occupations, and employers' reports of clients' satisfactoriness. They also concluded that research studies of the effectiveness of developmental guidance interventions on the whole suggest that developmental programmes can make an impact, but 'do not yet provide any firm empirical basis for affirming (or denying) the superiority of such programmes to the more traditional approaches' (Watts and Kidd,

1978). The tentative nature of these conclusions reflects the paucity of carefully conducted research which explicitly confronts the criterion problem described above. One of the major aims of the study we report in this volume was to examine the relative effects of exposure to the currently popular developmental approach to careers guidance in the light of the criticisms which have been levelled at it.

Research on the Transition from School to Work
In only a handful of studies in Britain has an attempt been made to study the transitional process as a whole, and even within these, serious methodological weaknesses sometimes make interpretation of the results difficult, and practical policy recommendations nearly impossible.

Carter (1962) carried out a longitudinal study of transition from school to work between 1959 and 1960 using a sample of 200 school leavers from the Sheffield area. The adolescents in the sample were interviewed three times. The first interview was held early in the last term of school; the second interview was held three months after the respondents had left school; and the third interview took place one year after they had left school. The interviews focussed upon a number of different areas including attitudes towards school and leaving school; jobs aimed at and jobs obtained; methods of finding jobs; job changing; attitudes towards work, co-workers and supervisors.

This comprehensive and detailed survey provided a rich source of descriptive material about the decisions, situations, events and experiences which arise during the transitional phase. Carter concluded from an examination of schools and the Youth Employment Service that both were achieving only limited success in helping adolescents during this period of their lives, and were in a large measure, failing. The study indicated that this failure stemmed from the inadequate allocation of resources in these institutions. In the years since Carter's study, social and economic conditions in Britain have obviously changed dramatically, and it is therefore important that detailed study of the transition from school to work, in current conditions, be carried out anew. Furthermore, whilst there are important details of overall trends, the precision and framework provided by statistical examination of results is lacking in Carter's study. We therefore see a need for up-to-date studies in this area, employing both subjective and objective data and utilising statistical testing, in order that a more accurate appreciation of the transitional phase may be obtained. Similar disadvantages of lack of detailed analysis and inapplicability to the contemporary problems of adolescents leaving school, apply to the study carried out by Veness (1962) and to the Crowther Report (1959). One of the more recently reported studies (Maizels, 1970) would appear to be less subject to the latter disadvantage, but even this research was carried out as long ago as 1965. Maizels' study however, does incorporate more detailed statistical analysis than previous studies, and covered a wide range of subjects including leaving school; attitudes to teachers and schools; sources of vocational help; vocational aims and attainments; job changing; attitudes to work and supervisors. Maizels concluded that there were wide discrepancies between the needs and opportunities of school leavers, and argued that it was the nature of role allocation in society which underlay the 'evident failure of the educational and vocational guidance services, and of industry, to fulfill the needs of more than élite minorities, whose abilities, attitudes, and aspirations are such as to allow them to make effective use of the services which exist and to respond to the opportunities available' (Maizels, 1970). One major criticism of the study carried out by Joan Maizels is that it involved the use of a retrospective questionnaire design. Retrospective studies involve asking individuals about events which occurred in their past or attitudes which they held in the past. The reports that people give about their past experience however, are notorious for errors of omission and distortion and such reports can therefore be of only limited value.

    Maizels interviewed 183 boys and 147 girls who had left school in the previous three years and who were employed in the Willesden area of London. She also conducted interviews with their employers in order to obtain a comparison of the views of employers and young workers. As we have said much of the data gathered was retrospective, and descriptions particularly of leaving school and choosing and finding employment therefore require the validation that a longitudinal study can provide.

THE ACADEMIC ORGANIZATION OF SCHOOLS

Many studies have examined selected aspects of the transitional phase and study of each of these aspects has inevitably raised theoretical questions, often with important underlying policy implications, but always the questions raised by the controversy over occupational choice theory, have been most keenly debated and discussed. In setting up the present study therefore, we were concerned that we should be able to compare the occupational aims and attitudes to work of school leavers who had been exposed to contrasting philosophies of careers education. The difficulties of securing co-operation of subjects and organizations for research purposes are well-known in the field of social sciences, and we were very fortunate, therefore, to gain the co-operation of two schools in very similar catchment areas. In one of the schools a developmental approach to careers guidance was employed, whilst the other followed a more traditional 'differentialist' (square pegs into square holes) philosophy of careers education and guidance. We then found that the two schools also differed dramatically in their organizational structure. One school adopted a banding system in which half of the students were assigned to the 'A' band and the other half were assigned to the 'B' band. 'A' band pupils were those considered academically bright and 'B' band pupils were thought to be less able. The other school was run along broad 'mixed ability' lines with a mixture of abilities in classes being the general rule. This fortuitous discovery enabled us to extend the investigation beyond the originally intended aims, into an area which has excited both popular and academic debate.

Research on streaming and mixed ability methods of teaching has shown that, on average, there are no differences between academic attainment in streamed and unstreamed schools (Passow et al, 1967; Barker Lunn, 1970; Jencks et al, 1975). However, within streamed schools, children in the higher streams tend to exceed children in the lower streams in scholastic attainment, by a margin greater than would be expected on the basis of differences in initial ability and social class background.

Lacey (1970, 1974) examined the effects of streaming in a grammar school and concluded that much of the energy and drive towards academic achievement is 'frittered away because the effects of relative failure in the competitive process are allowed to demoralise a large section of the competitors'. Lacey argued that the development of an anti-academic sub-culture is encouraged by streaming, and that competitive academic strivings are socially unacceptable within those sub-cultures. In a follow-up study of the same school after it had changed to mixed ability groupings, Lacey found that the less able had improved their exam performance, whereas the change made no difference to the exam performance of the most able groups. In another study, Postlethwaite and Denton (1978) found evidence of better overall performance on the part of less able pupils from the mixed ability situation, without lowering the overall levels of attainment achieved by the more able.

Barker Lunn (1970) in a study of streaming in Junior Schools, found that young children of average and below average ability became more motivated to do well in non-streamed schools. In a follow up study of the sample in Barker Lunn's study, Ferri (1971) found that by the end of their second year in secondary school, there were no differences in academic attainment between those who had attended streamed and those who had attended unstreamed Junior Schools. Finally, studies carried out in the USA by Jencks et al, (1975) led them to conclude that whilst mixed ability groupings were preferable, 'desegregating schools internally would not have much effect upon students' test scores'.

The effects of streaming upon academic attainment do not therefore appear to be quite as dramatic as some would argue. Of at least equal importance however, are the social effects for streaming upon children's attitudes and behaviour, and far less research attention has been directed towards this area. Postlethwaite and Denton (1978) found that pupils from mixed-ability backgrounds in Banbury school had better attitudes towards the school as a social community, while attitudes to the school as a working community seemed not to be affected by early grouping differences. Moreover, they found that these differences in attitude were particularly marked among the girls. Pupil participation and integration in Banbury school as a social community was higher in the case of children from the lower socio-economic groups, if they were from a mixed-ability system. Postlethwaite and Denton argue that children from higher socio-economic backgrounds would be less likely to have favourable attitudes to the school, if they found themselves to be in a mixed-ability system. They reasoned that the parents of such children would be suspicious of an environment different from that in which they gained their own education, and would be likely to influence their children's attitudes accordingly. Barker Lunn's (1970) study of Junior Schools suggested that attitudes to school varied with ability: pupils of lowest ability holding the least favourable attitudes and the brightest pupils holding the most favourable attitudes. In both streamed and unstreamed schools, children of below average ability had the poorest relationships with teachers, the poorest academic self-images and the worst social adjustment. Also, children of this ability level had poor school-related attitudes which Barker Lunn explained as a consequence of their limited academic ability. In general, poor school-related attitudes appeared to be exacerbated by teachers' attitudes. Streaming was also an important factor however, since children in streamed schools took less part in school activities than those in non-streamed schools. This difference was particularly striking among children of average and below average ability, and from lower social class backgrounds. In the follow-up survey of the sample, Barker Lunn (1971) found that pupils in unstreamed secondary schools played a greater part in school activities, thereby providing some confirmation for her earlier results.

Hargreaves (1967) found that in streamed schools, pupils in higher academic streams interacted together more and developed a more academic orientation. They had more commitment to the academic values of the school and staff, and tended to be critical of those who rejected the establishment's norms. In contrast, pupils in lower streams developed their own norms of behaviour and had a counter culture rejecting the academic strivings of the higher stream pupils.

There is therefore some evidence from a number of different sources, that streaming in schools has an effect upon the social organization of schools, and upon the attitudes and experiences of the pupils within them. However, there is almost no research which relates school organization to the transition from school to work. Swift (1973) has examined the differences in the experiences of grammar school and secondary school boys in the transition from school to work. Effects due to school organization in this study cannot therefore be distinguished from effects attributable to academic ability and social class background. Given that attitudes and experiences are influenced by school organization, it remains a possibility that attitudes and experiences during the transition phase might be similarly influenced. We therefore determined to assess whether such things as occupational aims, attitudes to work, attitudes to supervisors and hopes and expectations for the future, might be affected by school organization. Another area of possible investigation was differences in the transition from school to work between boys and girls.

SEX DIFFERENCES IN THE TRANSITION FROM SCHOOL TO WORK

In recent years there has been increasing discussion about curricula differences for boys and girls, since boys tend to be more often steered towards science and vocational subjects than do girls. Differences in socialising processes also encourage markedly different behaviour and traits in girls and boys, and produce differences in their aspirations and expectations. Later, in working life women are discriminated against - for example, it is generally more difficult for women to gain promotion or to be appointed to senior positions (Hunt, 1975). The combination of such influences can be expected to lead to radical differences for boys and girls in the methods and routes of their passage from school to work. It might well be for example, that girls are more disillusioned on entering work for the first time, if the world of work is less rewarding and more confining for women. Gove (1972) has suggested that the status accorded to women in working life can have harmful effects upon their self-image, and even their mental and physical health. The possibility that socialising processes and work practices are contributing to ill-health among women is disturbing, and more research attention is now being devoted to this question (See for example, Kopp, 1979).

The transition from school to work is an apposite phase in development at which to examine sex differences in working life, since it usually marks the first entry into work. Initial reactions and expectations can be measured to provide a more accurate picture, largely uncontaminated by previous experiences. Examining the experience of females alone, of course, provides little information about the relative importance of findings, and it is therefore vital in a study of this kind to compare data gathered for both males and females. An important aim of the study described here was to

15

examine in detail the differences in experiences, attitudes and ambitions, between males and females leaving school and starting work.

THE STUDY

The study was designed to explore many different aspects of transition from school to work, including the issues described above, and was carried out in two mining communities in Nottinghamshire, England, which we chose to call Woodbank and Brookvale. Both communities are situated within ten miles of a major city, and regular bus services operate between the city and the two communities. Both towns are traditional mining communities, which provide job opportunities in textiles, wood-machining and light engineering. Brookvale also provides some job opportunities in agriculture and is surrounded by fields and woods. Woodbank and Brookvale are very similar in most respects.

The Schools
Woodbank school was formerly a technical grammar school, and retained a large core of staff from this period. The school had 1400 pupils at the time the study was conducted and it made use of two sites, so that 850 pupils in the third, fourth and fifth years and in the sixth form shared one set of buildings. The other building was perceived by those in our sample as a much more friendly place and many regretted leaving to come to the new building which they saw as more impersonal. Woodbank school was rapidly expanding at the time of our survey, and the headmaster and many members of staff believed strongly in a 'banding', or streaming system, and students were assigned to the 'A' band or the 'B' band during the third year. Within the bands, all subjects were assigned to a higher or lower stream but the system of banding was a superordinate structure, dividing the school into those who were academically bright and those who were not expected to be academic successes. There was also an unofficially declared policy of assigning teachers to 'A' or 'B' band classes on the basis of their qualifications, the better qualified teachers being responsible for teaching 'A' band classes. Students in the 'A' band were encouraged in academic pursuits, and were usually entered in any GCE examinations in which they had a reasonable hope of success. Those who had some hope of

achieving passes in Advanced level GCE examinations were usually counselled to stay on at school beyond the age of 16. The timetable was arranged so that many 'A' band pupils were unable to take vocational options. Careers teaching was also limited for them to one half hour a week - both because of the perceived importance of examination subjects, and the questionable assumption that these students needed less vocational guidance than their counterparts in the 'B' band. In contrast, students in the 'B' band were perceived as failing academically, and as requiring extensive vocational guidance. Although some students in the 'B' band took examinations, they were usually CSEs, and there appeared to be relatively little concern amongst staff about the number of examinations 'B' students took. Careers teaching for this group was one hour per week, and students were occasionally allowed time off from school to search for jobs or to participate in work experience programmes. They were far more likely than students in the 'A' band to be involved in visits to potential places of work.

Brookvale school was smaller than Woodbank, with only 780 pupils in the five years. It was formerly a secondary modern school (both schools having become comprehensive in the three years prior to our study) and, like Woodbank, it retained a nucleus of its previous staff. Academic expectations were much lower in Brookvale, for although a majority of students took some CSE examinations, only a handful were likely to try for any more academic qualifications. Furthermore, Brookvale did not incorporate a sixth form, though there were plans for expansion in this direction in future years. There was no official streaming or banding system in Brookvale, classes generally being organized along mixed ability lines. Some department heads, however, did group students according to ability. In Brookvale, careers guidance was considered very important for all students in the school. In the third and fourth years, 35 minutes per week were given to careers, while in the fifth year, 70 minutes each week were devoted to careers teaching. Careers visits were scheduled relatively frequently for those who were leaving full-time education in the fifth year, although these visits tended to cater more for boys than girls. The average level of educational ability amongst the pupils who constituted the fifth forms, was roughly equal across the two schools.

Careers Education
The philosophies of careers education in the two
schools formed a sharp contrast. The careers teacher
in Woodbank was a vigorous proponent of Super's
(1957) approach to vocational guidance. He was very
concerned with the psychological growth and development of his students and endeavoured to build self-
awareness, self-confidence and trust among them.
He was determined that students should realise that
the responsibility for finding jobs was theirs, and
he was therefore loath to arrange job interviews or
to suggest jobs to individual students. His lessons
were always informal and frequently involved the use
of unfamiliar materials and encouraged students to
evaluate their attitudes and experiment with new
ideas and possibilities. He talked with students
individually about what they had done to find jobs,
but clearly left the initiative and responsibility
with them.
    At Brookvale, the careers teacher had a more
traditional approach to his job. He was familiar
with the local job market and went to great efforts
to place students in jobs for which he felt they
were suited. His advice was closely tied to the
local opportunity structure, and he was less concerned with the expressed wishes of students if
he thought that they were unrealistic. In his
classes the lessons were more formal than the
Woodbank careers lessons. He tended to concentrate
on interviewing skills, methods of job applications,
letter-writing skills, technicalities associated
with employment such as wage slips, National
Insurance contributions and so on. He related
to his students in a paternalistic way, whereas
the Woodbank careers teacher tended to be more
informal and friendly with pupils. In contrast
again, he went to considerable efforts to arrange
job interviews, and tended to see his job as one of
finding and placing his students in jobs. It was
apparent, that neither careers teacher saw giving
detailed information about jobs and working life as
an essential and primary element in their work.
In the case of Woodbank school, self-awareness and
choice were stressed, whereas Brookvale pupils were
taught some of the technicalities of working life
and were placed, wherever possible, in available
jobs.

The Interviews
Defining the period over which the transition from
school to work occurs is inevitably arbitrary. It

could be described as the period from the last day at school until the first day of work. Alternatively, it could be defined as the time from when individuals first begin to think seriously about getting a job, to the time when they decide that they are happy and settled in their work. We have chosen to define the period as stretching from about 6 months prior to the date of leaving school, to 30 months after the date of leaving. Accordingly, we interviewed 174 school leavers (86 boys and 88 girls) within 6 months prior to their leaving school. Ninety of the pupils were from the fifth form of Woodbank, and the other 84 were from the fifth form of Brookvale school. Of the Woodbank pupils, 52 were from the 'A' band and 38 were from the 'B' band.

The first interview was designed to elicit vocational preference, knowledge about jobs and the means of getting jobs, opinions of careers interviews, parental wishes, and attitudes towards teachers and school. Other information related to expectations of the future of the adolescents, attitudes towards sex roles, and demographic data including parents' occupations, family size and position of respondents in the family. This first interview was conducted at the schools, and each interview required approximately thirty minutes.

Nine months into their working life, an effort was made to contact all of those who had co-operated in the first interview. We were able to contact 103 adolescents (48 males and 55 females; 52 ex-Woodbank and 51 ex-Brookvale pupils) and they were again interviewed at the schools. These interviews lasted approximately forty five minutes each and the adolescents were asked a wide variety of questions about their experiences since leaving school and starting work. Information was elicited about examination passes; attitudes to the careers service; length of time involved in finding the first job; methods used to find jobs; help received from the schools and the careers service in finding jobs; job changes and reasons for job changes; attitudes to work, supervisors and co-workers; experiences on starting work; training required for jobs; pay and conditions; changes in home life and attitudes to society.

The final interview could not be conducted by teams of interviewers because of the logistical problems entailed in contacting all of the original sample, and arranging for them to meet in one place. A short questionnaire was therefore posted to all of those who had participated in the interviews conducted at the school shortly before they left. Ninety-three returned the questionnaire completed, of whom 47 were males and 46 were females. Forty-nine former Woodbank and 44 former Brookvale pupils completed and returned the questionnaire. The questionnaire was designed to provide details of the adolescents' experiences and attitudes after 2½ years of working life. They were questioned about current jobs; how settled they were in the jobs; opinions in retrospect of help received from the schools and the careers service; number of job changes and reasons for job changes. At this time (2½ years after the beginning of working life), we were also able to contact and gain information about the current jobs and job histories of a further 61 of the original respondents. This gave us up-to-date information on the job histories of 154 of the original 174 respondents.

At all stages of the study, the adolescents were generally co-operative and friendly, and appeared willing and keen to help us by providing all the information they could.

The results gleaned from the many interviews with the adolescents, their teachers and employers in the areas, provided us with a huge fund of information to draw upon when we came to examine the various areas of transition from school to work. In particular, the information gave us the exciting opportunity of exploring the issues of effects of school organization upon transition; sex differences in experiences during transition to work, and the effectiveness of contrasting methods of careers education.

Chapter Two
ATTITUDES TO TEACHERS AND SCHOOLS

There is good reason for believing that examination of the attitudes of pupils to their teachers and their schools is relevant to our understanding of adolescent development. Firstly, there is evidence that children's attitudes to teachers and schools are related to academic achievement. Jordan (1941), Arvidson (1956), Shinn (1956) and McGauvran (1955) have reported finding relationships between pupil attitudes and academic success. Pupils with favourable attitudes to school tend to be more academically successful. Barker Lunn (1971) found that in her study of primary schools two factors emerged as important correlates of a child's attitudes to schools. The child who had a positive attitude to school tended to have a satisfactory teacher relationship and to attach a certain degree of importance to doing well in school. Barker Lunn also found that when the teacher expressed dislike for the least able pupils, the class as a whole tended to reject these pupils. However, when the teacher accepted the least able pupils and exhibited no discrimination against them, the class as a whole did not reject them. Research in social psychology would lead us to suppose that pupils' attitudes to teachers and schools will be much affected by the attitudes their teachers have towards them.
    Secondly, attitudes to school are affected by school organization. We have described in Chapter 1 how streaming in schools affects the attitudes and experiences of the pupils within them. Hargreaves (1967) has shown that there is a social division between those in higher and lower streams in streamed schools, and it would be of some value to examine differences between streams in attitudes to teachers and schools. Surprisingly, very little has been done to examine the relationship between

teachers and pupils. Most studies examining attitudes of pupils towards their teachers and schools have been designed to elicit pupils' stereotypes of 'good' and 'bad' teachers (Bush, 1942; Michael et al, 1951; Allen, 1961; Taylor, 1962). These stereotypes may only represent mythical caricatures rather than reflections of pupils' real attitudes towards their teachers. It is therefore important to elicit pupils' attitudes to their own teachers as real and immediate persons. Joan Maizels, in her large scale study of transition from school to work (Maizels, 1970) did this by using a check list adopted from a National Institute of Industrial Psychology study (Handyside, 1961). She administered this check list to a sample of adolescents who had recently left school and was able to compare attitudes to teachers with attitudes to supervisors at work. The findings from her study are discussed below.

This leads us to a third reason for examining attitudes of pupils to their teachers and schools. It is a well-established finding that the rewards used by teachers, the manner in which this power of reward is used, and the content of teaching, can all have long term influences on pupils out of school and in later life. The relationship between teachers and pupils therefore has implications for pupils' attitudes and expectations both in the short term and in the long term after they have left school and started work. It might be, for example, that attitudes held by pupils to school may form a pattern which they then copy on leaving school and starting work. It may be that regardless of ability, those pupils who hold unfavourable attitudes to school would hold similarly unfavourable attitudes towards work organizations. In the same way attitudes towards teachers may be generalised towards all of those who hold authority in the workplace. Thus supervisors may be viewed by young workers in much the same way as they once viewed their teachers. This possibility has been investigated by Maizels who found that views about supervisors were 'almost identical' with those about teachers, though teachers were more frequently criticised than were supervisors. Maizels' analysis however is only cursory and it is difficult to assess the strength of the relationship she reports between views held about teachers and views held about supervisors. Furthermore, her study was retrospective in that young workers were asked to state their views about teachers after they had left school. We hoped to considerably extend Maizels'

work by examining pupils' attitudes to teachers and then, after pupils had left school, compare these attitudes with their attitudes to supervisors. Furthermore, we wanted to discover whether differences between groups of pupils in attitudes to teachers later manifested themselves, after they had left school, in attitudes to supervisors.
A fourth reason for examining attitudes to teachers and school arises out of our interest in the sex differences in transition from school to work. Teachers exercise a considerable influence on their pupils' attitudes and expectations and are a powerful force in the process of sex role socialization. Girls' attitudes and experiences might be shaped at least partially by their relationship with their teachers. Douvan (1979) found evidence of sex role norms operating in the behaviour and expectations of teachers and in the official reward system of American high schools. For example, girls complained that their sports programme did not have the resources or backing from teachers comparable to the male programmes. Douvan argued that the message continually being put across to the students seemed to be that males warranted more resources because of the importance of school for their vocational futures. We might well expect that the effects of such messages would manifest themselves in sex differences in attitudes to teachers (if similar discrimination exists within British secondary schools).
For these reasons therefore, we hoped to be able to discover something about the relationship between the attitudes of pupils to their teachers and schools on the one hand, and academic ability (as measured by CSE and 'O' level passes), school organization (a streamed versus an unstreamed school), attitudes to work and supervisors and sex of pupils, on the other.

Attitudes to Teachers
The pupils in both Woodbank and Brookvale were interviewed shortly before they left school and were presented with cards on which statements such as 'good to work for', 'sarcastic', 'moody', 'encourages me' were printed. Each student was invited to choose the items which described the teachers at school, and each was told to choose as many items as he or she wished. This checklist of descriptions was the same as that used by Maizels (1970) and, like Maizels, we have divided the statements into those which were favourable (e.g. 'explains things

clearly', 'full of ideas'), and those which were
unfavourable descriptions (e.g. 'have favourites',
'too young') of teachers. Also some statements were
seen as describing personal characteristics of
teachers (e.g. 'too old', 'kind') and some as describing professional or work-related characteristics
(e.g. 'explain things clearly', 'don't seem
interested'). The percentages of the pupils
choosing favourable and unfavourable items are shown
in Figure 1 (see also Appendix A). There was a
highly significant and positive correlation between
the results of the present study and the results of
Joan Maizels' survey. This suggests that the scale
we used is reliable. However, it would be wrong to
assume that the adolescents' responses to these
items represent an objective assessment of existing
pupil-teacher relationships. It may well be, for
example, that teachers in the two schools did praise
more than 16.7% of pupils when they did well, or that
pupils and teachers had different criteria upon
which good work was judged. What the data do show
however, is that a majority of pupils appear to
perceive their teachers as helpful and fair people,
but that only a small proportion perceive their
teachers as good to work for, clever, or full of
ideas. Only a small percentage perceive teachers as
being sincere people. (5.7%). Just under half the
adolescents in the present survey described their
teachers as having favourites, and one quarter of
the sample described their teachers as moody and
sarcastic.

It is more encouraging, at least from the
teacher's point of view, to find that adolescents
are more likely to describe their teachers in
favourable than in unfavourable ways overall. Of
more interest, however, is the finding that they
tended to express their favourable perceptions more
in relation to teachers' personal characteristics
than they did in relation to professional characteristics. Conversely, their unfavourable perceptions
appeared to focus more on professional characteristics. In Maizels' (1970) study, favourable
perceptions tended to be more mixed between professional and personal items, but she also found that
school-leavers tended to be more negative about
teachers' professional characteristics.

Differences between schools
There were clear-cut, significant differences in
attitudes to teachers between the two schools
(Table 1). The pupils in Brookvale were consistently

Favourable Items | Unfavourable Items

24.5% 31.0% 21.2% 14.9%

Professional characteristics

Personal characteristics

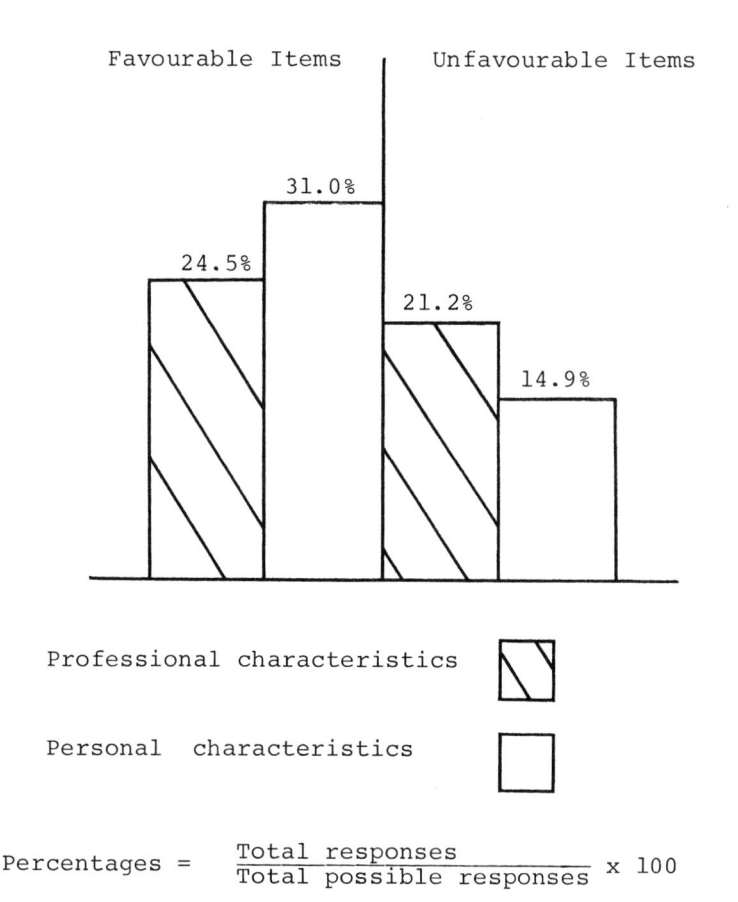

Percentages = $\frac{\text{Total responses}}{\text{Total possible responses}} \times 100$

FIGURE 1 Percentages of pupils choosing items to describe teachers' professional and personal characteristics

more favourable about their teachers in terms of both personal and professional characteristics. Moreover, the pupils in Woodbank were consistently more unfavourable in their descriptions of their teachers, again both in terms of personal and professional characteristics. In particular, the pupils at Brookvale perceived their teachers as listening to what they said, good to work for, clever, helpful and kind, much more than did their counterparts at Woodbank. More of the pupils at Woodbank, on the other hand, appeared to perceive their teachers as expecting too much, not interested, sarcastic and moody, and more often chose the item 'you never know where you are with them' than did the pupils at Brookvale.

Differences between bands
Within Woodbank school we found significant differences in the ways in which the 'A' bands pupils described their teachers (Appendix A). 'A' band pupils described their teachers more in favourable terms than did 'B' band pupils, and particularly in relation to personal characteristics (Table 2). For example, the 'A' band pupils were much more likely than 'B' band pupils to describe their teachers as fair and sincere, and a higher percentage of 'A' band students felt that they were treated like human beings by their teachers. 'A' band students also tended to describe the teachers at Woodbank as efficient, likely to encourage pupils, and likely to listen to what pupils said.

More 'B' band pupils described the teachers as nagging, strict and expecting too much. The pattern as a whole was for 'A' band students to describe the teachers at Woodbank significantly more favourably and slightly less critically than 'B' band pupils.

It is a possibility that these differences between Woodbank and Brookvale in attitudes to teachers could be entirely due to the 'B' band students in Woodbank. Comparisons between them revealed that the students of Brookvale school were more favourable and less critical than 'A' band students of Woodbank, in their descriptions of their teachers. However, the differences between these two groups of pupils were not significant and may have arisen merely by chance. This suggests therefore that much of the difference between the schools may be explained by the predominantly less positive and more negative descriptions of teachers given by 'B' band students in Woodbank school.

TABLE 1 Percentages of respondents choosing items to describe teachers in the two schools

	Favourable Items		Unfavourable Items	
	Woodbank School	Brookvale School	Woodbank School	Brookvale School
Professional Items	23.3	25.8	27.6	25.8
Personal Items	26.8	28.6	24.9	23.5

TABLE 2 Percentages in the 'A' band and 'B' band of Woodbank School choosing items to describe teachers

	Favourable Items		Unfavourable Items	
	'A' Band	'B' Band	'A' Band	'B' Band
Professional Items	23.9	20.8	22.8	22.7
Personal Items	26.3	25.4	17.0	19.1

TABLE 3 The relationship between descriptions of teachers and educational ability. Figures represent average number of favourable and unfavourable descriptions of teachers

Number of exam passes	Favourable Descriptions	Unfavourable Descriptions	Number of Pupils
None	5.0	3.5	21
1-3	4.9	2.3	21
4-6	6.4	2.1	36
7 & over	5.4	2.6	24

27

The more obvious explanation for the differences in attitudes to teachers between the 'A' band and the 'B' band is that attitudes to teachers may vary with the ability of students. Barker Lunn (1970) for example found that amongst primary school children, in both streamed and unstreamed schools, children of below average academic ability had the poorest relationships with teachers. Children of above average ability tended to have the best teacher relationships. It might be therefore, that the differences between bands which we found, could be due to a variation in attitudes with educational ability. To test this possibility we compared exam passes of all pupils in the sample at CSE and 'O' level, with attitudes to teachers (Table 3). It can be seen from the table that there was no relationship between descriptions of teachers and exam passes, though pupils with 4-6 examination passes tended to be the most favourable and least critical in their descriptions of teachers.

As there was no relationship overall between attitudes to teachers and educational ability, we are led to the conclusion that the system of banding employed within Woodbank school had an important effect upon students' attitudes to teachers. Specifically, pupils allocated to the 'B' band, and thereby labelled as academic failures, had significantly less favourable attitudes to teachers. Our research suggests that unfavourable attitudes are not associated with lack of academic success per se, but that they are associated with the labelling which is a consequence of the formal identification and differentiation of an academically unsuccessful group within the school. There is no evidence that streaming is a significantly better way of organizing schools for improving average academic performance, but we have found evidence of damaging social effects within schools of this method of academic organization. We referred earlier to the work of Jordan (1941), Arvidson (1956), Shinn (1956) and McGauvran (1955) which showed that there were relationships between pupil attitudes and academic success. Our findings would suggest that a system of streaming is likely to produce unfavourable attitudes to teachers amongst those placed in lower streams, and other research has shown that these unfavourable attitudes may militate against academic success regardless of educational ability amongst pupils in lower streams.

Sex differences
In our sample, we found that the boys were significantly more favourable in evaluations of their teachers than were the girls (Table 4). They were more likely to describe their teachers as efficient, good to work for, reliable and sincere. For example, out of 88 girls in the sample, only one described her teachers as sincere. On unfavourable items relating to personal characteristics the girls in the sample were significantly more negative, tending to describe teachers as sarcastic and nagging.

As there was a larger proportion of girls in Woodbank than in Brookvale, differences between responses of girls and boys between schools, were compared. It might have been that the slightly different proportion of sexes in the schools was responsible for the overall differences in attitudes to teachers between schools. The girls appeared to be less favourable and more critical in descriptions of teachers, and Woodbank pupils were less favourable and more critical than Brookvale in their evaluations. Comparisons of responses of boys between the two schools, revealed a consistent trend for boys in Woodbank to be less favourable and more critical than their counterparts in Brookvale. The same was true for the girls. The differences in attitudes to teachers between schools were therefore consistent, even when the factor of sex was controlled.

There was no significant effect of social class of pupils (as determined by social class of father) in evaluation of teachers.

Attitudes to schools
To elicit descriptions of schools another checklist of items was presented to the adolescents, and again they were asked to choose the items which described their schools. As in the attitudes to teachers scale, the items on the checklist can be divided into favourable and unfavourable items (Maizels, 1970) (Appendix A). There were twice as many favourable references overall to schools as unfavourable references, and more than half the pupils in the present survey described their schools as offering a good standard of education (Figure 2). A large proportion of the students also chose the items 'up to date', 'friendly' and 'has a good reputation' to describe their schools. Over 40% of the respondents however appeared to feel that a lot of lessons seemed a waste of time.

TABLE 4 Percentage of girls and boys choosing items to describe teachers

	Favourable Items		Unfavourable Items	
	Boys	Girls	Boys	Girls
Professional Items	27.7	21.5	22.1	20.3
Personal Items	31.8	30.2	12.0	17.9

TABLE 5 Attitudes to leaving school held by boys and girls

	% Boys	% Girls
Very keen to leave	29	12
Keen	24	21
Not bothered	26	21
Sorry	18	37
Very sorry	3	9

Differences between schools
The differences in attitudes to teachers between pupils from Woodbank and Brookvale schools were reflected in the pupils' attitudes to their schools (Figure 3). The students of Brookvale were more favourable in their descriptions of school than the pupils of Woodbank school. Less than 40% of Woodbank students described their school as offering a good standard of education, but 65% of the Brookvale students chose this item. This is a surprising finding given the fact that Woodbank had formerly been a technical grammar school, whereas Brookvale school had been a secondary modern school, prior to the change to a comprehensive school. It may be that students in Woodbank viewed the change as a change for the worse whilst the opposite may have been true in Brookvale. This would also explain why over 60% of the Brookvale pupils we interviewed, appeared to feel that their school had a good reputation, whereas only 32% of Woodbank repondents described their school in this way. Nearly half of the Brookvale pupils also described their school as 'just the right size', whilst only 27% of Woodbank pupils chose that item. This difference may be related to the fact that Woodbank was bigger than Brookvale and whilst both schools were expanding, Woodbank may have already been perceived as too big by the pupils.

For every negative item but one, a higher percentage of Woodbank pupils than Brookvale pupils responded. Woodbank students appeared to feel that teachers were 'only interested in the brainy ones' and, perhaps not surprisingly, the 'B' band students within Woodbank chose this item more than any other group within the sample (e.g. males, females, social classes 4 and 5). Woodbank students also appeared to feel their school was too big, and both 'A' band students within Woodbank and pupils of high socio-economic background from both schools, chose this item most often.

A consistent picture of more positive and less negative attitudes to school and teachers in Brookvale school is thus painted by these results.

Sex, band and social class differences
There were no significant differences in attitudes to school between bands in Woodbank school or between sexes. The 'B' band tended to describe Woodbank as more friendly, strict about time keeping, and having too many rules and regulations. The 'A' band, conversely, saw the school as too big, not

having enough discipline, needing fresh people at the top, providing too little practical training and as easy going. There were few differences between the responses of boys and those of girls, though boys appeared more likely to see school as efficient and having a good reputation. The girls appeared to see school more as a friendly place than did the boys.

Pupils from high socio-economic backgrounds (Classes 1 and 2) were less favourable about the schools than pupils from social classes 3a and 3b, and those from social classes 4 and 5. The adolescents of social classes 1 and 2 were less likely to see the school as helping everyone to do their best, as having a good reputation, as friendly and as just the right size. This finding may be related to the recent changeover of both schools to comprehensive systems. The attitudes of parents of higher social class background are less likely to be favourable towards comprehensive schools, which are radically different from the system of schooling they received themselves. Their attitudes are also likely to have a considerable influence upon the attitudes of their children towards their schools.

Liking for school
One question in the interview tapped the adolescents' feelings about school more directly. They were asked 'how well do you like school?' Overall, 59% of those who replied to this question reported some definite liking for school ('like school very much' or 'like school quite a lot') and 24% reported some definite dislike ('do not like school very much', 'do not like school at all'). There were no differences between the two schools in liking for school on this question but the girls in the sample did seem to like school more than the boys. Within Woodbank, a higher percentage of 'A' band pupils indicated their liking for school than did 'B' band students. The difference between the bands was particularly marked in relation to expressions of definite dislike. Only 16% of 'A' band students said that they did not like school very much or did not like school at all, compared with over 30% of the 'B' band pupils. A comparison of expressed liking for school with number of exam passes revealed no significant relationship, again supporting the explanation that banding rather than educational ability was the important factor. Proportionately more adolescents from social classes 1 and 2 expressed definite liking for school than those from

|Favourable Descriptions|Unfavourable Descriptions|
39.7%
19.8%

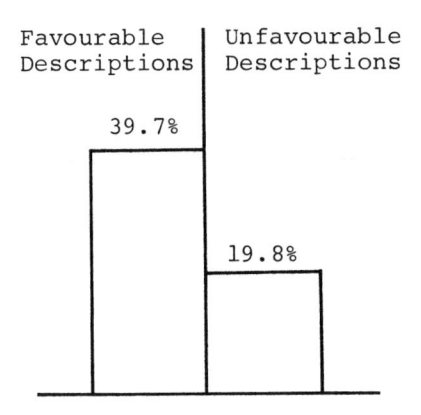

FIGURE 2 Percentages of favourable and unfavourable items chosen by pupils in their descriptions of schools

|Favourable Items|Unfavourable Items|
46.0%
33.8%
25.1%
15.2%

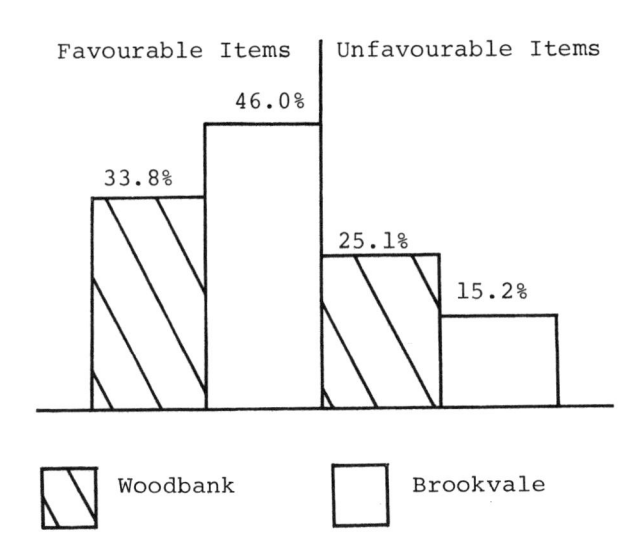

◸ Woodbank   ☐ Brookvale

FIGURE 3 Percentages of pupils in Woodbank and Brookvale schools choosing items to describe their schools

social classes 3a and 3b, and least liking was indicated by the replies of adolescents from social classes 4 and 5. These findings appear anomalous when compared with the finding of more favourable descriptions of school amongst those from lower socio-economic backgrounds. It may be that such children would be less likely to criticise school if they found it to be a rewarding social institution but would be more likely to find the regulations and formal organization of the school restrictive, given their relative lack of academic success. The reverse would then be true for those from higher socio-economic backgrounds.

Leaving school
The students in the survey were also asked how they felt about leaving school, and they could answer in one of five ways: 'very keen', 'keen', 'not bothered' 'sorry', 'very sorry'. Just over half (57% of the respondents expressed some inclination to leave school (very keen or quite keen to leave) and 24% expressed some sorrow at leaving (sorry to leave or very sorry to leave).

The girls in our sample were less keen and more sorry than the boys to leave school, and this difference was highly significant (Table 5). There was no significant relationship between school and attitudes to leaving, though a larger percentage of Woodbank pupils expressed some sorrow at leaving school (Woodbank: 38%; Brookvale: 29.3%).

Nine months after leaving school and starting work all those contacted in the follow-up survey were asked how much good they thought that their last year had done them, and what they thought the lowest school leaving age should be. Almost 60% felt that the last year had done them either a lot of good or some good, and only 13.7% felt that their last year had done them no good at all. Sixty percent of the pupils felt that the school leaving age should be kept at 16 years, and less than 30% felt it should be lowered to 15. Given that the school leaving age was raised only 2½ years before this survey, it is interesting to note how rapidly the pupils appeared to have accepted the change.

School Life vs Working Life
In the follow-up interview, nine months after the adolescents left school and started their working lives, they were asked 'All things considered, are you happier now than when you were at school?' Just over 66% felt they were either a bit happier or

much happier since leaving school (48% indicating they were much happier). Just over 10% felt a bit less, or much less happy since leaving school. There were no differences between the two schools in the responses to this question, but girls were significantly less happy at work. Only 58% of girls were happier at work compared with 77% of boys (see Figure 4), and 18% responded to the question by indicating that they were less happy than they had been at school, compared with only 2% of boys. This finding is consistent with other attitudes expressed by the girls in their working lives.

Summary of Results
Overall the adolescents we interviewed were more likely to describe their teachers in positive ways, though some negative items, such as 'sarcastic', 'moody' and 'have favourites' were chosen by a high proportion from among the items available to them. There were also twice as many favourable references to schools as unfavourable references. Schools were described as offering a good standard of education, being up to date and friendly. Many pupils felt that a lot of lessons were a waste of time and felt that there was not enough practical training. The majority of the pupils appeared to like school very much or quite a lot, though an identical percentage (57%) were quite keen or very keen to leave school. Most (60%) felt that their last year of school had done them some good and that the lowest school leaving age should be kept at 16.
   Over two thirds of the adolescents reported that they were either much happier or a bit happier after leaving school. Only 10% felt less happy since leaving school.
Schools:- the pupils of Brookvale were much more favourable in their descriptions of their teachers than the pupils of Woodbank. The latter were more unfavourable in their descriptions of the teachers. In the descriptions of the schools the same trends were evident.
Bands:- within Woodbank school, the 'A' band pupils described their teachers in much more favourable terms than did the 'B' band pupils. 'B' band pupils were slightly more unfavourable in their descriptions of their teachers than were the 'A' band students.
Sex differences:- the boys were significantly more favourable in their evaluations of teachers than were girls. The girls were significantly more unfavourable than the boys in their evaluations of teachers' personal characteristics, describing them as sarcastic

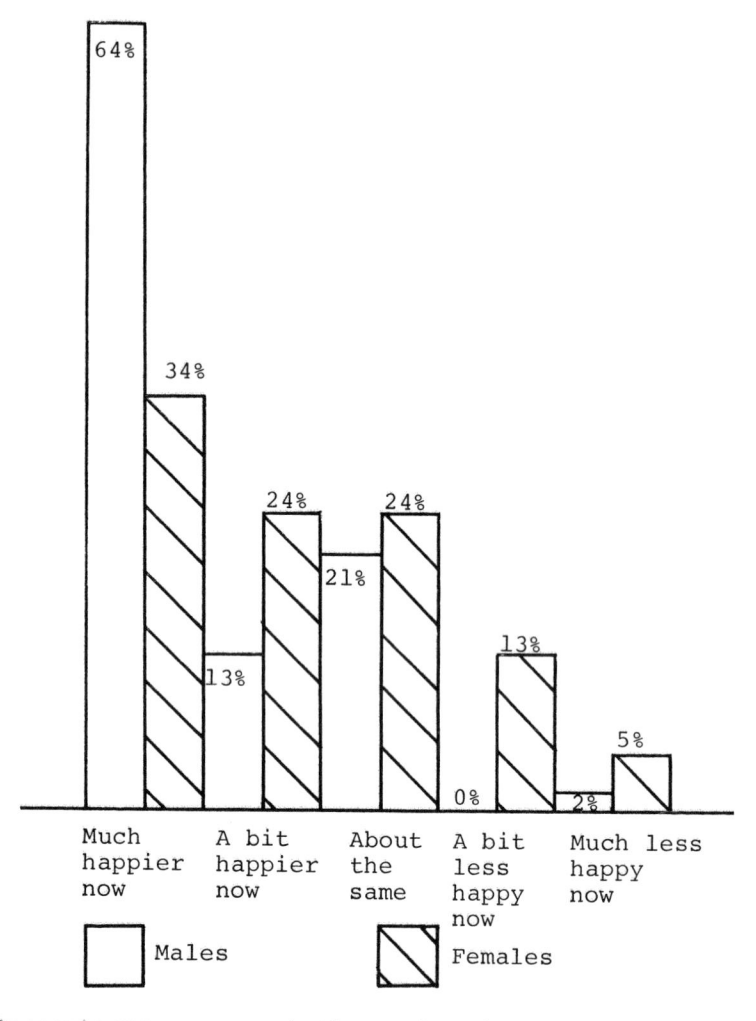

Bar chart showing:
- Much happier now: Males 64%, Females 34%
- A bit happier now: Males 13%, Females 24%
- About the same: Males 21%, Females 24%
- A bit less happy now: Males 0%, Females 13%
- Much less happy now: Males 2%, Females 5%

☐ Males ◨ Females

Percentages represent those choosing each category in answer to the question ' All things considered, are you happier now than when you were at school?'- nine months into working life

FIGURE 4   Attitudes of males and females to working life compared with school life

and nagging. When asked directly, the girls appeared to like school more than the boys and were significantly less keen to leave school. Having left school and started work, they were much less happy than they were at school, in comparison with the boys.
Social Class differences:- adolescents of higher social class backgrounds were more critical in their evaluation of schools than those from lower social class backgrounds. Paradoxically, adolescents from classes 1 and 2 expressed more liking for school than those from social classes 3a, 3b, 4 and 5.

Conclusions
The consistent pattern of unfavourable attitudes to teachers and school amongst the pupils of Woodbank indicates that the ethos within the two schools we studied, differed markedly. It is difficult to explain this difference in terms of catchment areas served by the two schools and to argue that the two groups of pupils differed at intake since the areas served by the schools were very similar. A more plausible explanation is that the difference reflects the differences in academic organization and academic emphasis in the two schools. Woodbank placed more emphasis upon academic achievement and retained a banding and streaming system, so that about half of the students (who were considered academically brighter) were placed in the 'A' band streams and the other half were placed in the 'B' band streams.

Hargreaves (1967) has shown how the organization of schools into academic streams affects social relations within schools. Willis (1978) found a sharp distinction between the cultures of lower stream pupils who rejected the school's norms ('the lads') and their counterparts ('the ear 'oles) who tended to conform to the values of teachers. Hargreaves found that the higher the stream, the more favourably the pupils regarded the teachers. In the 'A' stream in his survey the pupils were positively orientated towards the teachers' values, liked them and had better relationships with them. This finding is replicated in our survey - 'A' band pupils being significantly more positive in their evaluation of teachers. The fact that there was no relationship between exam passes and attitudes to teachers and schools suggests that the differences between the bands was an effect of banding and not an effect of educational ability.

Apart from these banding differences within Woodbank, the pupils of the school were still significantly more negative than the pupils of Brookvale overall. It may be that this difference can be entirely accounted for by the perpetuation of streaming. Hargreaves (1967) has suggested that streaming produces stereotyped hostile attitudes between the streams, and it is likely that the overall level of conflict within a school, can be increased by creating a large group alienated from the teachers and the school system. Certainly, 'A' band students saw Woodbank as not having enough discipline and as being 'easy going', where 'B' band students described the school as having too many rules and regulations and as being strict about time keeping. The pattern of results suggested that for 'B' band pupils school was important as a social community. At school they met their friends and 'messed about' and derived gratification from the fun and friendship of school rather than from the content of lessons. Rules and regulations were an irksome part of school life for them. It appeared that they wanted to leave school as quickly as possible but while they were there, they gained satisfaction from the social content of their school lives. 'A' band students on the other hand saw the school as too 'easy going' and requiring more discipline. For them, school was a place of work which they attended in order to gain knowledge and examination passes which would stand them in good stead when they began work. This opposition of goals and cultures within schools has been colourfully portrayed in Willis' (1978) book Learning to Labour. Amongst others, Finlayson (1973) has emphasised the mental health of pupils and the degree to which their emotional and social development is fostered in school. It may be that a system of banding does produce attitudes of rejection of authority and hostility within schools and the possibility is one which needs careful investigation. It is not an outlandish possibility given Rutter et al's (1979) conclusion that: 'to an appreciable extent children's behaviour and attitudes are shaped and influenced by their experiences at school and, in particular, by the qualities of the school as a social institution'.

Differences between sexes appear more complex than the differences between the schools. On the one hand, the girls were significantly more negative and less positive than the boys in their evaluations of their teachers, and on the other, they liked school more than the boys, and were less keen to leave. Having left school, they were significantly less happy at work than were the boys.

Allen (1961) found that girls comment rather less favourably on school than boys but an examination of the comments on which his findings were based, reveals that they are almost all comments relating to teachers, and so our findings are consistent with Allen's. What Allen also found was that girls' favourable comments about teachers showed a significant decline between the first and fourth years at secondary school. Allen concluded that if girls mature more rapidly or sooner than boys, they may feel that discipline is geared to a lower level of maturity than their own. Another explanation is that the effects of sex role socialization in adolescence come to affect attitudes to teachers during adolescence. Studies of the self concept in adolescence suggest that academic achievements become less important for girls that they do for boys (Douvan, 1979). Intelligence and passing exams are devalued for adolescent girls and they appear more concerned with being popular and good-looking. For boys, the reverse appears to be the case - as they move through adolescence boys appear to become more concerned with academic success and to develop their vocational aspirations. Girls' changing attitudes may then be reflected in their attitudes to teachers, whose academically-orientated values are alien to the norms and values of the adolescent female's world. There is some evidence that girls - especially those of above average ability - develop a poorer self image and become more anxious during adolescence (Ferri, 1971). Shaw (1976) has also shown that girls are led to expect less from school life than boys and this may contribute to their alienation from the academic norms of teachers.

An alternative explanation is that teachers use different techniques of social control in the classroom for boys and girls. De Groat and Thompson (1949) carried out a study of the distribution of teacher approval and disapproval amongst 6th grade pupils in America and found that teachers give more approval to the brighter children and expressed more disapproval towards the less able children. They also found that girls had fewer contacts overall with their teachers. Serbin et al (1973) looked at the way teachers responded to disruption by pupils in the classroom, and at the way they responded to 'dependency' (crying, soliciting attention and trying to be near the teacher). This study was carried out in American nursery schools. Again, it was found that, overall, teachers responded much more to boys. They were more likely to respond to aggressive behaviour in boys (a trend noted previously by Meyer and Thompson, 1956) and to boys' solicitation of their attention. The rate of teacher attention to children who were participating in class activities without being disruptive or dependent, was higher for boys. The probability of teachers responding to boys who were participating in classroom activities without being disruptive or dependent was more than one and a half times greater than the probability of them responding to participating girls. Finally, praise was given more often to boys than to girls. Such a catalogue of bias is by no means restricted to male teachers. De Groat and Thompson (1949) found that even female teachers tended to have far fewer contacts with girls in the classroom than with boys.

Ireson (1978), in a review of the research, concluded that girls were rewarded at nursery school for staying near the teacher, rewarded in primary school for social achievements in school, and reprimanded in ways that emphasise their academic incompetence when it occurs. It is of course questionable whether the American experience parallels that of British schools, but we have no reason to doubt that similar patterns of student-teacher interaction occur in both countries. As girls mature through adolescence they may become more aware of the sharp differences in the way teachers behave towards male and female pupils. If they interpret the lack of attention and praise as rejection then it is hardly surprising that girls should describe their teachers in less favourable ways than do boys.

This does little to explain why girls appeared to like school more than did boys. The girls in the sample described the school as a friendly place and were much less keen to leave. An explanation for this can be found in the importance attached to different characteristics during adolescence. Adolescent girls are more accepted by their peers if they are popular and socially successful. So school would be more important for social achievement and for the expression of social strivings through making friends, being with friends and participating in group activities, than it would be for academic achievement. Therefore, for adolescent girls, school may be important and valuable to them as a social institution and less important as an educational institution. This might explain why they should like school and yet, at the same time,

hold relatively unfavourable attitudes towards teachers.
In conclusion the results of the examination of attitudes of pupils to teachers and schools, provides illuminating data which also suggest, given the correspondence between our results and Maizels' findings, that the scales of measurement we used can be reliably employed with different samples of pupils. Our research sample was such that we were able to examine some schools and group differences, and this showed that attitudes to school and teachers can differ markedly even within one school, according to the group or category tested. It would therefore be useful to extend this research to an examination of attitudes in different types of school - co-educational, single sex, comprehensive, grammar, in different areas, amongst children of different ages and in different groups within schools. Given the internal consistency of the results of this survey, it may be possible to evaluate in more detail the effects of different types of school organization and climate upon school-leavers' attitudes to school and teachers, and to suggest ways of improving the relationship between pupils, and specific groups of pupils and their teachers and schools.

Chapter Three

OCCUPATIONAL CHOICE

During the process of growing, learning and developing, children and adolescents are asked with greater and greater frequency 'What do you want to be when you grow up?' Early in childhood this question is relatively unimportant in the individual's life,but, during adolescence, finding an answer to the question becomes a more urgent task. Adolescence is also a stage of life when individual identity is of greater concern and so decisions about occupational choice become inextricably linked with the individual adolescent's view of himself or herself. Adolescents 'struggling to decide on their future occupations and careers are, in a sense, engaged in the process of defining themselves as adults in the world' (Richardson, 1978).

But decisions about occupational choice are important not only for their influence upon identity, for they can also have significant implications for the adult's future happiness and adjustment. When people are unhappy in the work they have chosen, this unhappiness is likely to affect their overall levels of satisfaction and happiness in life(Crites, 1969). The work we do also determines our social status and is likely to have a significant effect upon our attitudes, hopes and expectations. Occupational choice therefore represents perhaps the first major choice that a young person has to make in life, and this choice is likely to have profound effects upon later experience.

Not surprisingly, a variety of professionals are concerned with occupational choice processes. Occupational psychologists, sociologists, economists and careers guidance counsellors all have an interest in the processes by which adolescents choose their jobs. The range of factors and influences which have been proposed as important in the choice processes, has ranged from those located in the individual, to those located in the wider social system (see Chapter 1 for a review of theories of occupational choice). Personality, educational experiences, home background, talents, interests and sex have all been shown to be of importance, but equally, existing economic climate, available job opportunities and locale have been examined and research evidence shows that these factors also, are undoubtedly of some importance in the processes of occupational choice.

In order to see the complex area of theoretical approaches to occupational choice more clearly, it is useful to clarify the many different theories into a smaller number of categories. Each of the theories reviewed in Chapter 1 can be classified in this way and can be seen as falling within one of three major perspectives on the occupational choice process.

The first approach, originating in the writings of Parsons (1909), has been called the 'differentialist' or 'matching' theory of occupational choice. Theorists from this school see individuals as having different abilities, interests and personalities, and view occupational choice as a process of matching these attributes with the requirements of available jobs. So, for example, Holland (1966) sees people as developing occupational choices out of a search for work situations which provide outlets for their values, interests, aptitudes, personality factors, intelligence and self-concepts. Roe and Siegelmann (1964) stress the contribution of early parent-child relationships to later adult behaviour and occupational choice. Job satisfaction for the individual, according to these theoretical approaches will depend on the congruence of job requirements and the personality or attributes of the individual.

Developmental theorists on the other hand see the differentialists' models as too static. They prefer to describe occupational or vocational choice as a long process involving personal growth, and the development of awareness of 'self' and of preferred life style. Super, for example, has argued that the self-concept has a crucial influence in the process of occupational choice. According to Super, the whole process of vocational development is essentially that of developing a self-concept and then implementing that self-concept in vocational choice. These theorists also divide life into age stages and attempt to identify norms of vocational development for each age stage. Ginzberg, for example, has described an age stage of 'tentative choices' which spans the period of adolescence from eleven to seventeen years of age. During this time individuals are thought to become more and more aware of a need to find criteria by which their choices of occupations can be made and evaluated. Greater vocational maturity is thought to be reached as each stage is passed.

A third approach emphasises how the wider social system and 'opportunity structures' dictate occupational choice. Careers, according to this alternative theory (Roberts,1975), are seen as developing in ways dictated by the opportunity structures to which individuals are exposed - first in education and then in employment. Thus, children who attend educationally selective schools (e.g. grammar schools) are likely to have higher expectations of the world of work and more confidence in their own ability, than children who attend schools which are generally regarded as of low standard. Roberts talks of 'climates of expectation' which become associated with particular educational institutions. Thus, schooling is seen to have a profound influence upon children's aspirations. Then, having entered a particular occupation, individuals can only climb the career ladders which are available in the industries in which they find themselves. Individuals are thus seen as being subjected, even after entering employment, to socialising processes which shape their future occupational choices.

Choices, Preferences and Attainments
Some evaluation of these different approaches can be attempted by focussing on adolescents' occupational choices and discovering relationships with such factors as how long they have wanted the particular jobs they have chosen; how many jobs they have considered; and what reasons they give for the particular choices they make. In this chapter we shall describe the choices of the school leavers we interviewed, some of the reasons they gave for their choices, and the differences between groups (e.g. schools, sexes, bands) in the status of jobs chosen. It is important at the outset however, to stress that occupational choice is the object of our focus. Occupational attainments is altogether a different area of study. The relationship between occupational choices and occupational attainments is still poorly understood, but we do know that many adolescents do not succeed in securing jobs they choose to aim for,

while they are still at school. A distinction between choices, preferences, expectations, aspirations and attainments certainly needs to be made, because some of the disagreement between theorists in this area can be traced to a confusion of these terms. So, for example, Vroom (1964) speaks of preference - 'I should prefer outdoor work to indoor'; choices - 'I should like to become a transport driver, or a bus driver and not become a shop assistant'; and attainments - the actual occupation the individual ends up in (Wallis, 1978). It can be seen that the distinction between preferences and choices here is not entirely clear. Hoult and Smith (1978) on the other hand, define preferences as the job a person liked and could do, but for some reason would probably not attain; choice is defined by them as the jobs a person expects he or she will probably end up in; and aspiration is defined as a fantasy or dream job. The differences in these definitions and the idiosyncratic nature of some of them can lead to arguments over theory which have their bases in semantics. Accordingly, in our work, we have defined occupational choice in terms of the answers to the question which school leavers were asked: 'What job would you like to do when you leave school?'

RESULTS

Occupational Choices

All of the adolescents were asked the above question, six months before they left school, and the jobs they chose are shown in Table 1. Amongst the boys, the most popular choices were apprenticeships, with mining coming second. Amongst the girls, office work of some sort was the most frequently chosen occupation, followed by machining work in the textile industry. Other popular choices were jobs in the Forces, teaching, shopwork and engineering. More unusual choices ranged from professional footballer to airline pilot.

The occupations chosen by the school leavers in our sample were then classified according to their socio-economic status. Given the lack of specificity of some choices it was often impossible to use the Registrar General's Classification of Occupations. It proved more productive to apply a system with fewer categories, and accordingly the choices were classified according to Reiss' (1961) Occupation and Social Status Classification. The status of choices of pupils in Woodbank and Brookvale are shown in Appendix B and it can be seen that there is a highly significant relationship between status of occupations chosen and school. Pupils in Woodbank (the banded school) were more likely than those from Brookvale to choose higher status jobs (Table 3). Not surprisingly, within Woodbank the 'A' band students were more likely than 'B' band students to choose higher status jobs (see Appendix B).

The difference between the adolescents from the two schools in socio-economic status of jobs is unlikely to be the result of differing educational abilities or differences in samples, given the similarity of catchment areas and the similar sizes of the schools. Furthermore, there were no overall differences on socio-economic status of the backgrounds of children attending the two schools. It would seem more likely that differing careers guidance techniques or differences in school organization are responsible. Firstly, the careers teaching in Woodbank was based on the developmental approach to occupational guidance, which has been elaborated by Eli Ginzberg et al (1951). This approach emphasises occupational choice as being a result of the long process of personal growth and of the development of self-awareness through childhood. Advocates of developmental theory see individuals as translating their relevant beliefs about themselves into occupational preferences, through the matching of self concepts with information or beliefs about possible occupations. The teacher or careers officer subscribing to this theory, therefore plays a supportive but essentially non-directive role, only helping to deepen the individual's self-awareness and knowledge of her or his environment. The careers teacher at Woodbank encouraged his pupils to be aware of their likes, dislikes, attributes etcetera and encouraged them to find out about available jobs in the locality as well as in the nearby city of Nottingham. Decisions about occupations however tended to be left entirely to the individual. The careers teacher in Brookvale, on the other hand, employed techniques prompted by the differentialist or matching model, which were more directive than the techniques used by the Woodbank careers teacher. His approach, in its simplest form, involved assessing the individual's abilities and interests and matching them with available jobs until the best 'fit' was obtained. The careers teacher's aim was thus to guide the students into jobs he thought most suitable for them, based

TABLE 1 Occupational choices of respondents

OCCUPATION	NUMBER OF RESPONDENTS
Apprenticeships (e.g. Gas engineers, joiners, plumbers, fitters, vehicle mechanics etc.	31
Office work	25
Machinist (textile industry)	17
Mining	15
Forces	11
Teaching	11
Shopwork	8
Nursery Nurse	7
Engineering	7
Police	4
Nursing	4
Technician/Science Research	3
Business	3
Draughtsman	3
Cookery	2
Driver	2
Solicitor	2
Hairdresser	2
Embroiderer	2
Others (e.g. Economist, journalist, pilot, footballer)	11
Don't know	4
TOTAL	174

TABLE 2 Reasons given by school-leavers for their Occupational choices

CATEGORY		% OF TOTAL RESPONSES
'Inner-directed'	Likes, interest and abilities	39.5
	Interesting or exciting job	6.5
	Sub-total	46.0
'Tradition-directed'	Family member does it	26.6
	Friend does it	9.4
	Sub-total	36.0
'Other-directed'	Money	3.6
	Saw other, careers talks, etc	10.8
	Sub-total	14.4
Other	e.g. to move away, don't know	3.6
TOTAL		100.0

TABLE 3   Number of school-leavers from Woodbank
         and Brookvale schools choosing
         occupations of socio-economic Status 1
         to socio-economic Status 5

SOCIO-ECONOMIC STATUS OF OCCUPATIONAL CHOICE		WOODBANK SCHOOL	BROOKVALE SCHOOL
High	1	5	1
	2	26	7
	3	27	33
	4	17	30
Low	5	11	12

upon his knowledge of the students' abilities and interests, and his knowledge of local employment possibilities.

It may be, therefore, that the differences between adolescents in the two schools in the status of the jobs they hoped to get are explicable in terms of the differences in careers teaching in the two schools. It might well be that the 'developmental' approach encouraged students to be more imaginative and/or ambitious in their occupational choices. The students from Brookvale on the other hand, might see their occupational futures in more restricted and traditional ways, as a result of their exposure to the differentialist techniques of their careers teacher and their non-exposure to developmental techniques of careers guidance.

A second explanation derives from the differences between the schools in academic organization. Woodbank school employed a banding system separating pupils into academically able and academically less able streams. The effect of this may have been to somewhat heighten the expectations of 'A' band students for their working lives. Because they were viewed as academically more able (in comparison with 'B' band pupils) they may have anticipated rewards for this greater ability in the world of work, and assumed that one of these rewards would be higher status jobs. The findings that 'A' band students chose jobs of significantly higher status than both 'B' band students, and students from Brookvale school, add credence to this interpretation. However, 'B' band students at Woodbank, on average, chose jobs of higher status than those chosen by Brookvale pupils (though this difference was not significant). It is more difficult to explain this finding, since it suggests that the differences between the two schools cannot be attributed entirely to one band.

It may have been that the high expectations of the 'A' band were communicated to 'B' band pupils, who, though aware of their lower educational status, were in some way influenced by the climate of ambition within the school, to aim a little higher. This argument would propose that 'B' band pupils were affected by the ambitions of the 'A' band students so that the overall level of occupational aims within the school was raised. Alternatively, it could be argued that the 'B' band pupils were not prepared to accept the labels of 'educational failure' and 'low status worker' which were being thrust upon them, and were reacting to this

49

labelling by aiming higher. It could be argued that they were more determined to succeed in the occupational world, having 'failed' in their lives at school.

Whatever the explanations for these differences, the findings that occupational choices differ between schools, regardless of the academic ability of the pupils within them, is one which merits further investigation. It also suggests that some schools create more realistic expectations of the world of work than others, and this is an area of discussion we shall return to in Chapter 5.

Development of Occupational Choices

The adolescents were also asked how long they had wanted the jobs they had chosen, and there was great variation in the length of time that they had wanted particular jobs. From the point of view of developmental theorists, who see occupational choice as a long process of development towards the choice point, some of the results are difficult to explain. Nearly one in five (18.6%) had wanted the jobs chosen for less than 6 months, and over 40% had wanted the jobs chosen for less than a year. Over one in three, on the other hand, had wanted their jobs for 2 years or more.

No differences between schools or between sexes were evident in the responses to this question, but 'B' band pupils were more likely to have wanted jobs chosen for less than 6 months (25% of 'B' band children) than were 'A' band pupils ('A' band:11.4%). Similarly, only 5.6% of pupils from social class backgrounds classified (according to father's occupation) as 1 or 2, had wanted the jobs chosen for less than 6 months, compared with 20% of those from the other social classes.

These findings suggest that those from higher band and higher socio-economic status groups are more likely to have wanted their jobs for a long period of time.

Developmental theorists would argue that arrival at choices three, four and even five years prior to leaving school, indicates that occupational choice does involve processes which are in operation for some time, and that occupational choice is not a mere matching process that occurs when the time for decision making arrives. It is interesting in this light that the developmental theory has been criticised because it '.....resembles reality in the case only of those more privileged individuals who are able to make genuine career decisions'(Roberts,

1975). Our findings might therefore be viewed as offering some support for this criticism.

Number of Jobs Considered

Attempts were made to elicit details of all the jobs the school-leavers had considered or were considering, including even the jobs they had fantasised about during childhood, and the number of jobs each pupil mentioned was noted. We were astonished to find that over 40% of those we interviewed only remembered considering 3 or fewer than 3 jobs. Only 1 in 10 had apparently considered 6 or more jobs in their lives. This conservatism amongst school leavers in their exploration of the world of work is somewhat disturbing. It certainly belies any suggestion that young people are well-prepared for employment, in the sense that they have thought carefully about the opportunities open to them before choosing a particular job.

There were no school or sex differences in the number of jobs mentioned. The 'A' band within Woodbank school, however, mentioned significantly more jobs than did 'B' band children. There was also a highly significant relationship between academic ability (as measured by the total number of GCE and CSE passes) and number of jobs mentioned. In other words, those who did well academically at school were likely to have considered more jobs before arriving at their career choices than those who did not do so well. In relation to the discussion above about the developmental theory of occupational choice, it is interesting that adolescents from these educationally and socially higher status groups should have considered more jobs than children from other groups, in the process of arriving at occupational choice. One interpretation of this is that they saw more opportunities open to them and so, in a very real sense, were able to make a choice from among these alternatives. Again, this would suggest that the developmental theory of occupational choice is more applicable only to academically more able children.

The fact that overall, the school-leavers had considered few jobs by 15 or 16 years of age, should not be taken as a sign of apathy or fatalism amongst them about their future working lives. By the time we conducted the first interviews in the schools, six months before the pupils were due to leave, 97% of them had actively sought jobs by writing letters, telephoning or visiting firms. Some of them had made as many as 20 applications for jobs 6 months prior to leaving school.

Reasons for Occupational Choice
It is very important to check with school-leavers about their reasons for job choices, because their responses may provide additional clues as to how adolescents actually go about making their choices - what factors influence them most, whether these choices ultimately are just chance outcomes, which family members have more influence and so on. This information is also useful because it will tend to support, qualify or question the existing theoretical explanations of how adolescents arrive at their occupational choices. There is every need for these explanations to be sharpened if they are to be of value to those who seek to apply them to the 'real world' of the school leaver.

In an examination of reasons for job choices however, a number of problems arise. Firstly, the reasons given by adolescents for their job choices are varied and multiple. Some offer four or five different reasons where others offer only one. Furthermore, in an interview there is always the possibility that the adolescent may give the first answer she or he thinks of, or an answer may be given which is intended only to please the interviewer - the socially desirable response. Thus it would be unwise to accept unquestioningly that the reasons for job choice cited by school-leavers are the true determinants of their occupational choices. Nevertheless, they are of some value since they give at least a rough indication of reasons for job choices pertinent and perceptible to the individual school-leaver.

In two previous studies of the transition from school to work (Veness, 1962; Maizels, 1970), the investigators asked the adolescents about the reasons for their job preferences. In these studies, they found it useful in showing the emphasis placed by children upon different factors or influences, to employ a system of classifications originally used to describe different societies and the personality or character types they produce (Riesman,1950,1952). The categories in this system are 'tradition-directed' reasons; 'inner-directed' reasons and 'other-directed' reasons. We have duplicated the use of these categories because they proved to have the advantage of fitting and describing our results very well.

In using these categories to describe occupational choice, 'tradition-directed' describes reasons for choices determined by family or neighbourhood tradition, e.g. 'my mother does it'; 'I've got friends who work there'; 'my father works in the pit'. 'Inner-directed' describes reasons for choices based on the individual's likes, abilities and self-perceived talents e.g. 'I like biology'; 'I wanted to help people' (job choice of nurse); ' I like working with people'; 'I liked woodwork in school and I enjoy using my hands'. 'Other-directed' reasons for choices are those which are based on information or experiences which are essentially external. This can perhaps be better understood by comparing 'other-directed' with 'inner-directed' choices. 'Inner-directed' reasons for choices are based on interests, likes and abilities, whereas 'other-directed' choices include, for example, 'As a result of careers talks'; 'Seen it on TV and read in books'; 'Because of the good money'; 'Saw police in pub'. Veness (1962) describes 'other-directed' choices as: "those made with primary reference to outside sources of information, or to considerations of the chooser's position in the general social order..... The other-directed chooser is one who has been attracted by a talk or a pamphlet or by seeing a member of the profession at work..... or he may be primarily concerned with the prospects a job offers".

    The category 'tradition-directed' is particularly interesting from a theoretical point of view since it is not a reason for job choice that is easily accommodated by the developmental or differential theorists. If young people do choose jobs often only because of family or neighbourhood tradition, it suggests that Roberts' conception of opportunity structures might be expanded to include the family. The family might thus be seen as a structure which has a significant influence on the adolescent's occupational choice, and therefore the occupational histories of those within the family could be seen as forces, shaping the most likely choices for the adolescent. Thus the family would represent another structure (other than school and work organizations) which will tend to limit or expand the adolescent's opportunities. Certainly, in our survey, the 'tradition-directed' category of responses to the question 'How did you decide that you wanted to do this kind of work?' accounted for a substantial proportion of all the responses:

53

Family member does it		- 26.6% of responses
Friend does it	'Tradition-directed'	- 9.4% of responses
Interests, likes or abilities		- 39.5% of responses
Interesting job		- 6.5% of responses
Money		- 3.6% of responses
Other e.g. saw man doing it, seen on TV, careers talk etc.		- 14.4% of responses

It can be seen that these responses fall easily, for the most part, into the classification system adopted by Veness from Riesman's categories and which are shown in Table 2 (Page 47). Inner-directed reasons for choice were, overall, the most frequently offered, and within this category, the sub-category of 'interests, likes and abilities' included most reasons for occupational choice. Of respondents in this sub-category, 27% referred to liking of academic subjects as reasons for choices e.g. 'I like biology/woodwork/physics', and 73% referred to an aptitude or liking for a particular past experience as a reason, e.g. 'I get on well with young children'; 'I like office work'; 'I helped build a house extension and really enjoyed it'; 'I like babysitting'.

In Thelma Veness' and Joan Maizels' studies and in the present survey, inner-directed reasons accounted for the largest percentage of responses. However, in the present survey, tradition-directed reasons for choices were the next most frequent, and this differed from the findings in Maizels' and Veness' studies. In the studies they reported, this category accounted for the smallest percentage of respondents, other-directed reasons for choices being more frequently offered. A possible and plausible explanation for this difference in findings may be given in terms of the differences of locality of the studies. The present survey was conducted in two mining communities, near to but still separate from, a large city. Veness' survey was carried out in a number of differing areas, including towns in an agricultural district, seaside towns, a densely populated maritime district and a dormitory area of large housing estates near London. Maizels' survey was confined to the Willesden suburb of London. It is apparent that the mining towns chosen for our survey are much more likely to be characterised by community identity than disparate towns and villages and large London suburbs. The difference between these two previous studies and the present survey therefore, could well account for the difference in emphasis placed by school-leavers upon the influence of family and friends. If this is the case, and there prove to be very large differences in different regions in the processes of occupational choice, it is something that practitioners in the field such as careers guidance officers as well as employers, need to take account of. If some adolescents in close communities do choose jobs just because their parents have done them, then both the advantages and disadvantages of steering them away or towards these choices need to be carefully considered.

Finally, other-directed reasons for job choice centred mostly on advice from careers teachers and careers officers, and on interest aroused by seeing others doing the job that was chosen.

The results of this examination of reasons for job choice suggest, therefore, that many initial job choices are made on the basis of the individual's self knowledge and self awareness as the developmental theory claims (but still bearing in mind the proviso that reasons for job choice should not be accepted totally at face value), and that, in line with 'differentialist' theorising, there is some matching between jobs and the individual's interests, likes and abilities. At the same time, in some communities it seems that, at least for the educationally less able, jobs held by members of one's family or by friends are likely choices. It has been a consistent finding of a number of investigations (e.g. Carter, 1962; Jahoda, 1952) that advice and information provided by parents is most influential in children's choice of jobs. Given that parents' experience and knowledge may be limited to only jobs they have held, it is not altogether surprising that children often choose the jobs held by their parents. The need for occupational choice theorists to include this important influence in their theories is obvious.

SUMMARY

Occupational choice theories fall into three categories: differentialist, developmental and opportunity structure. An examination of occupational choices amongst school-leavers in the present survey revealed that children from the banded school, where

55

careers teaching was based on developmental theories, aimed at significantly higher status jobs than children from the unbanded school employing a differentialist approach. Within the banded school, students from the higher band chose higher status jobs than students from the lower band. Those from higher socio-economic groups and from the higher band had also wanted the jobs they had chosen for a longer period of time, and had considered more jobs in arriving at their choices, than those from the lower band and the lower socio-economic groups. This suggests that developmental theories of occupational choice are more applicable to the academically or materially more fortunate adolescents. Finally, reasons given for occupational choices centre on children's perceptions of their own interests, aptitudes and likes. Family members and friends doing a particular job was a reason for choice which also figured prominently.

It is worth reiterating that occupational choices are not occupational attainments, though there is undoubtedly some relationship between them. In describing occupational choices and reasons for choices, one is not therefore describing attainments. Between choice and attainment is the vital period when the adolescent leaves school, begins to look for work, discovers vacancies, applies for jobs and ultimately accepts a job offer. During this period some choices become attainments, some hopes are dashed, some compromises are made and, very often, the future quality and course of an individual's employment history is determined. It is to an examination of the process of finding employment, and an evaluation of the sources of help available to the school leavers in our survey sample, that we now turn.

Chapter Four

FINDING JOBS AND SOURCES OF HELP

Having decided on a choice of job, the school-leaver then has to act to implement this decision by applying for jobs and making use of the various sources of help available at this time. From the point of view of both those who wish to advise young people and potential employers, this is a crucial phase in the transition period. It is important to know how efficient school-leavers are at finding and applying for their first jobs, and what shortcomings and advantages they find in the services and sources available to give them help. For example, do they find the institutions set up to assist them, such as the Careers Advisory Service, a real aid? To what extent do family members and friends help them to get jobs, and how far are the schools a valuable source of advice and practical assistance?
The answers to these questions are useful not only to those who wish to advise school-leavers. They are also of interest to employers, who wish to be sure that school-leavers with particular qualifications and interests are aware of the requirements and content of specific jobs in industry. At a wider social and economic level, it is important that the best use is made of labour resources. If there is very little knowledge amongst young people about the characteristics of various jobs in industry and commerce, many will end up in jobs for which they are not best-suited, and which will be less likely to give them satisfaction. The working lives of many young people are shaped and given direction by the first job they take, and this fact lends enormous weight to the importance of an examination both of their methods of finding jobs, and their use of sources of help.
Research studies in the past have focussed

57

attention primarily upon the usefulness of sources of help to school-leavers, and not on methods used to find jobs. This attention has also been directed almost exclusively towards an appraisal of Careers Advisory Services, with a consequent neglect of examinations of the usefulness of schools. Perhaps more importantly, the influence of informal sources of help, such as the school-leaver's family and friends, has received only the most cursory attention, despite a growing acknowledgement of the significance of the influences.

Few quantitative studies have examined the methods used by school-leavers to find their first jobs. Yet, many careers education programmes stress the importance of methods. Adolescents are trained in how to write good letters of application for jobs; they are instructed in basic interview techniques; in more progressive programmes, school-leavers act out interview situations to give them practice for 'the real thing'; and practice in using the telephone is also included in some lessons. It is impossible to accurately judge the usefulness of this training, though it is obvious that many school-leavers are considerably aided by it. However, the relevance of these skills to the reality of finding jobs is questionable.

How many letter applications eventually lead to employment? Is the influence of a family member a more important factor in getting a job? Do different groups of school-leavers have different experiences in getting jobs? It many be, to take the latter question for example, that girls or less-qualified adolescents are more reliant on the influence of family and friends and that, for them, practice in writing letters of application is redundant. We certainly would not claim to have the answers to all these questions but our preliminary results, in conjunction with the results of previous research, may provide impetus for further research on this neglected aspect of the transition period.

FINDING JOBS

Previous research has produced fairly consistent results, showing that many school-leavers secure jobs fairly quickly and that many secure the first job they apply for. Maizels (1970), in a retrospective survey of the transition from school to work, found that half of the boys and two thirds of the girls in her sample, had obtained the first job for which they had applied, and about half of all the school-leavers in her sample had obtained their first jobs prior to leaving school. Similarly, Carter (1962) found that half of the boys and girls in his study had obtained jobs before they left school. About a quarter of the school-leavers in Carter's study in Sheffield were offered and accepted the first job they applied for. These findings suggest two obvious interpretations. Firstly, it may be that school-leavers are astute in their applications and are well-prepared for leaving school and starting work. The second, and more likely explanation, is that economic conditions in 1962 and 1970 meant that the transition from school to work was a much easier process. The all too real threat of unemployment is a constant worry to school leavers in the 1980s, and the results of these earlier studies are probably no longer representative. To some extent, the same could be said of our survey, which, whilst it was carried out between 1976 and 1979, nevertheless concentrated on less qualified school-leavers in an area of relatively low unemployment, in comparison with the United Kingdom as a whole. Nevertheless, our results are important since they do provide information about less-qualified school-leavers, who often have the greatest difficulty in securing employment.

When the adolescents were interviewed at their schools six months before they left school, 33% told us that they had already found jobs. Fifty four percent did not have jobs, and the remainder were either uncertain about what they wanted to do, or else were hoping to be accepted at Colleges of Further Education. At the time of the second interview, nine months after they had left school, a majority (55%) of the adolescents indicated that they had secured jobs by the time they had left school (See Table 1). Most of the others (31%) had found jobs within a month after leaving school. Within the bands of Woodbank school, 'A' band pupils who were looking for jobs, were significantly less likely to have secured jobs at the time of the school interview than 'B' band pupils. Only 21.7% of the 'A' band pupils had jobs, compared with 56% of the 'B' band pupils. This finding was supported and was highly significant in the follow-up interview at nine months after they had left school. Only 31.6% of 'A' band pupils had managed to find jobs by the time they had left school, compared with 75% of 'B' band pupils (Table 1). However, an analysis of the data on length of time to securing first job, revealed no relationship with academic ability

TABLE 1 Length of time taken by all respondents and by 'A' Band and 'B' Band pupils to secure their first jobs

Time	%'A' Band	%'B' Band	% All Respondents
When they left school	31.6	75.0	55.0
Less than 1 month after leaving school	47.4	21.4	31.3
Less than 2 months after leaving school	5.2	0.0	4.2
Less than 3 months after leaving school	5.2	0.0	4.2
Less than 4 months after leaving school	10.6	3.6	5.3

Table 2 Number of job applications by school-leavers before they were given their first jobs

	%'A' Band	%'B' Band	% All Respondents
Applied for first job only	31.6	42.9	32.3
Applied for 2-4 jobs	21.0	39.3	33.3
Applied for 5-9 jobs	15.8	7.1	16.1
Applied for 10 or more jobs	31.6	10.7	18.3

overall, as measured by total number of exam passes. These band differences therefore appeared to be related to some factor other than academic ability. Hargreaves (1967) has shown that different types of secondary schools and the streams within them, inculcate in pupils beliefs about their abilities and expectations for their futures, which are based partially upon their allocation to a particular stream: " 'A' stream pupils develop a sense of superiority over the others, who, aware of their implied inferiority, come to regard the 'A' stream boys as 'snobs'." (Hargreaves, 1967). Ashton (1973) has also discussed the development of different frames of reference amongst youngsters and concluded that academically more able pupils are: 'systematically offered and pointed toward the promise of a greater reward in the short term future.' In the banded school we studied, over half of the pupils had been placed in the 'A' band, not all of whom could be expected to acquire jobs of significantly higher status than 'B' band pupils. However, 'A' band students were found, on average, to choose jobs of significantly higher socio-economic status than 'B' band students within Woodbank (see Chapter 5), suggesting that many were looking for 'a greater reward'. It is probable, therefore, that the relative delay in securing jobs experienced by those in the 'A' band of Woodbank school was a result of their significantly higher occupational aims, which could not so easily be fulfilled in the existing labour market. For many 'A' band pupils, between the time they had stated their occupational aims and secured their first jobs, there must have been a gradual changing of aims to the point where the aims could be fulfilled (Over 60% of 'A' band school-leavers were unable to secure the jobs they had originally aimed for - see Chapter 5). It appears, therefore, that adolescents unrealistically pointed towards the promise of greater reward, are likely to experience more difficulty than others in securing their first jobs. Overall, those of greater academic ability did not experience more difficulty in getting jobs. This suggests that it was less qualified adolescents who had been given higher expectations by their placement in the 'A' band, who suffered the longest delays in getting first jobs.

One alternative explanation for these findings should be mentioned. It is possible that jobs of higher status require longer application procedures such as letter writing, followed by interviews and eventual employment. Lower status jobs may be gained by just a telephone call. Therefore 'A'band students may have experienced a delay in getting jobs because of the more lengthy application procedures which are often associated with the kind of jobs for which they were applying.

APPLYING FOR JOBS

Previous studies which have examined methods of applying for jobs (Carter, 1962; Maizels, 1970), have produced differing estimates of the number of job applications adolescents have to make, before finding their first jobs. Carter (1962) found that about one quarter of those in his sample had applied only for their first job, but, at the same time, nearly 30% of those seeking work had applied for five or more jobs. Maizels (1970) however, found that over half of the boys and just under two thirds of the girls had obtained the first jobs for which they had applied. Less than one fifth had tried for more than three jobs before finally obtaining work. Again it is necessary to caution against generalizing from these results, given the vastly different economic conditions which exist today.

In the present survey, 32% of school-leavers who were seeking work obtained the first job for which they applied, though some 18% had to apply for 10 or more jobs (Table 2). There was a significant relationship between the bands within Woodbank school, and the number of job applications. 'A' band students made proportionately more job applications than those from the 'B' band. This highly significant finding probably reflects the fact that 'A' band pupils applied for higher status jobs, for which there was more competition. There were no significant relationships between number of job applications and schools, sexes or social classes. However, there was a significant relationship between examination success and job applications, those with more exam passes applying for more jobs. Again, this relationship can be explained by the fact that there is generally more competition for higher status jobs, and that those with examination successes are more likely to pursue higher status jobs. It is also possible to propose two equally likely alternative explanations. Firstly, it may be that those of higher academic ability have more choice in the number of jobs open to them, and therefore are able to make more applications, simply because there are more jobs which they can reasonably hope to be offered. Secondly, it is possible that applications are the more appropriate methods of securing jobs of higher status, and that informal methods (e.g. calling at a factory to see if there are any vacancies) are more appropriate for jobs of lower status. If the latter interpretation is correct then it would be predicted that those with more examination passes would report making more job applications.

Inevitably, number of job applications and the probability of success of each application varies between individuals (e.g.if an individual repeatedly applies for very high status jobs, chances of success will be reduced). In areas and times of high unemployment, job applications are less likely to meet with success, particularly in schools where expectations are raised. It would be interesting to discover how much the number of job applications made by school-leavers, varies with local and national unemployment figures. In our survey, the success of first applications may have reflected the relative ease with which school-leavers were able to find jobs. Indeed, 42.5% reported that there were other jobs they could have taken. Similarly, it was relatively easy for adolescents to find jobs in Sheffield at the time of Carter's study (1962), and for the children in Maizels' sample looking for work in London. It would be useful if similar analyses of the job applications of young school-leavers could be carried out in areas of high unemployment, so that comparisons might be made. Adolescents in different areas could then be given some idea of how persistent they might have to be in order to find jobs. It appears not uncommon, even in times of relatively low unemployment, for some adolescents to have to make 10, 20, 30 or even more applications, in order eventually to find work.

SECURING EMPLOYMENT

In order to gain some additional insight into the young workers' feelings about their first jobs, they were asked why they thought they had been given their first jobs. The answers to the question fell into a number of distinct categories (Table 3). Most of the adolescents felt it was something to do with their personal qualities or performances e.g. the impression made in the interview, exam results, etcetera. A large percentage (nearly one in four) did not know why they had been given their first job, and nearly a fifth reported that they thought the firm 'just had vacancies' and were 'desperate for people'. We were surprised to find that a relatively small number gave 'influence' as a reason for being given the job, despite the fact that family and friends were undoubtedly important sources of help in securing jobs for the young people (see below). Carter (1962) uses the term 'influence' to describe the ability of a person to make use of special connections in order to arrange a job for a school-leaver. In his study 'influence' was the decisive factor in securing employment for as many as one quarter of the boys and one fifth of the girls. 'Influence' is undoubtedly a factor in the search for work and though it cannot always be measured accurately, its importance can be inferred at least partially from the number of times it is mentioned informally as a decisive factor. In our survey, 'influence' appeared to be a decisive factor in many cases - a finding we shall return to below.

The young workers in the first follow-up survey, nine months after they had left school, were also asked whether they thought their classes at school (e.g. typing, woodwork, French, etc.), or their qualifications had helped them in getting jobs. Fifty eight percent thought not and only 27% thought that they had definitely helped. Within Woodbank school, qualifications and classes were reportedly more helpful to 'A' band students than they were to 'B' band students. This finding is not altogether surprising, and is consistent with the fact that 'A'band students were likely to leave school with more qualifications than 'B' band students. In addition, they would undoubtedly be more likely to see qualifications as important and instrumental in securing jobs, because of the time and energy they had invested in gaining them. It is interesting though that there appeared to be no significant relationship between the number of exam passes an individual had, and his or her perception of the helpfulness of classes and qualifications in gaining jobs. This suggests that the system of banding employed in Woodbank, may have inculcated in 'A' band students the assumption that school qualifications would enable them more easily to get jobs in the labour market. In other words, their expectation of the value of qualifications, may have led them to believe that qualifications helped them to get jobs. This belief was not shared by those who gained more exam passes in the whole sample. So, once again, the influence of the

TABLE 3   Responses to the question: 'Why do you think you were given the job?'

CATEGORY	% OF RESPONDENTS
Capabilities, made good impression, did well in test, good interview	40.1
The firm were desperate, had a number of vacancies, needed people	18.2
Worked there prior to leaving school	4.7
Only applicant	4.5
Knew someone working there	5.7
Don't know	22.7
Other	2.3
N = 88	100.0

TABLE 4   Responses to the question: 'How did you hear about your job?'

CATEGORY	% OF RESPONDENTS
Family	24
Friends	30
Careers Advisory Service	19
Newspaper	20
Other	7
N = 96	100

TABLE 5   Responses to the question: 'Did you get any help from the school or the Careers Advisory Service in finding this job?'

Yes/School	9.5
Yes/Careers Advisory Service	22.9
No	67.6
N = 105	100.0

banding system employed at Woodbank, appeared to be important in shaping the expectations and experiences of pupils who had attended that school.

SOURCES OF HELP

Having left school and started work, the young people were asked how they had heard about their jobs, and over half indicated family or friends as the sources of information. The Careers Advisory Service was mentioned by less than one in five of the young people in the sample (Table 4).

These findings,coupled with the results of previous research, suggest that the official services are useful in finding jobs for only a minority of school-leavers. Carter (1962) found that in Sheffield, only one in four of school-leavers were placed in their first jobs by the official service. Other studies (Jahoda and Chalmers, 1963; Maizels, 1970) vary in their estimates of the usage of official placement services between 30% and 32%. When asked whether they were helped to find their first jobs by either their school or the careers service, two thirds of the respondents in our survey indicated that they had not received help from these sources (Table 5). This result further reinforced the feeling that official services were helpful for only a minority. However, there is always a possibility that answers to global questions tend to distort the true picture, or to hide information that more probing questioning would reveal. We therefore determined to focus more closely on what appeared to be the most important sources of help: the Careers Advisory Service, the schools, family and friends and work experience.

1. The Careers Advisory Service

One of the advantages of a longitudinal study is that appraisals of sources of help can be compared at different stages of the transition from school to work. Thus, we were able to examine school-leavers' attitudes to the Careers Advisory Service and the schools as sources of help, firstly while the respondents were still at school, and again nearly three years later.

Out of 168 adolescents, 133 described the interview they had had with the careers officer at school as 'useful'.The interviews appeared to be occasions when information about where to apply for jobs was given. Many respondents mentioned that the Careers

Officer gave practical help in the form of addresses, telephone numbers or pamphlets relating to the school-leavers' job interests. Some students reported that the Careers Officer suggested specific jobs and 'suggested what would suit me'. Indeed, the nature of comment on the interviews with the Careers Officer was generally positive:

> 'Encouraged my choice'; 'made me less nervous about being interviewed'; 'helped me make up my mind and put me on the right track'; 'gave me ideas, information and suggestions'; 'helped to clarify things for me'; 'asked me what I wanted to do and what I was interested in'.

There were some unfavourable comments, but these were often from adolescents who were very definite about their future intentions, or who had no idea of what jobs to apply for:

> "The interview was a waste of time'; 'it was useless'; 'just tried to put me off the job I wanted'.

At 2½ years into their working lives, the young workers were again asked to assess the help they had been given by the Careers Advisory Service in finding a job. The results are shown in Table 6. It is encouraging to find that 30% of respondents found the Service helpful, but, at the same time, disquieting that over one third of respondents found the Service unhelpful or ineffective. There was still a certain amount of favourable comment:

> 'Told me where to go for the job I wanted'; 'put me in the right direction'; 'gave good information on all jobs, nothing was too much trouble'; 'they understand your personal feelings about something you will be doing for years'; 'they help you in finding out all the necessary information about exams required'; 'gave me addresses'; 'seemed very helpful and interested and gave me some useful addresses'.

However, the overall weight of comment on the Careers Advisory Service was critical:

> 'Gave me no help or guidance'; 'offered low paid and uninteresting jobs'; 'helped me look for jobs that didn't suit me'; 'tried to

TABLE 6 Retrospective assessment of help from the Careers Advisory Service in finding jobs - 2½ years into working life

CATEGORY	% OF RESPONDENTS
Helped a lot	10.2
Was helpful	19.3
Was good but could have been better	8.0
Was unhelpful	9.1
Made no difference	26.1
Didn't use it	27.3
N = 88	100.0

TABLE 7 Helpfulness of school in giving information about different jobs - six months before leaving school

CATEGORY	% OF RESPONDENTS
Very helpful	22.4
Quite helpful	58.8
Not helpful	17.0
Other	1.8
N = 170	100.0

TABLE 8 Retrospective assessment of help from school in finding jobs - 2½ years into working life

CATEGORY	% OF RESPONDENTS
Helped a lot	4.5
Was helpful	10.1
Was good but could have been better	24.7
Was unhelpful	19.1
Made no difference	41.6
N = 89	100.0

persuade me to do something different'; 'by the time they came up with a job, I'd already got one'; 'they tried twice to get me the job I have now, before I tried on my own and succeeded'; 'they showed a lack of personal interest and tried to talk me into a job with limited prospects'; 'they tried to force you to take jobs'; 'gave you the first job on their list whether you were interested or not'; 'told them what I wanted, they just wrote it down and that was that, I never heard from them again'.

It has been claimed that clients' reported satisfaction with careers guidance received, is a less 'objective' measure of effectiveness than studies of diagnostic accuracy, diagnostic guidance interventions and developmental guidance interventions (Watts & Kidd, 1978). And indeed, the biggest single problem in evaluating the effectiveness of careers guidance, lies in determining the most useful criteria upon which to base measures of effectiveness. Some researchers have used occupational satisfaction as a criterion, and others have used the extent to which the occupation entered was concordant or discordant with the guidance given. Criteria have included job-changing, self-ratings of suitability for jobs, employers' ratings of suitability, clients' knowledge of local job opportunities and the range of factors use by school-leavers in forming their job preferences. As Watts & Kidd point out, clearer specification of the aims of guidance is needed before the real effectiveness of guidance can be assessed.

Discussion about the aims of careers guidance inevitably leads to arguments about the aims of education: 'Are we preparing children to become grist for the mills of profit-maximising capitalists?' 'Should careers guidance be aimed at directing young workers in sufficient numbers to the industries that need them?' 'Should the educational system be geared to the changing demands of industry?' 'Should careers guidance be aimed at finding jobs for youngsters, which enable them to fulfill their potential?' 'Is it right to send young people into boring, low paid and dirty work?' 'Should education be about making the individual aware of him/herself in the broader context of existence, life, death, and moral and spiritual development, or should education be directed towards producing the most efficient labour resources to promote national economic growth?'

The answers of different theorists in the areas

of occupational choice, careers guidance and education, are often implicit in their theories. There is a wide range of answers to questions about the purpose of formal education, and these answers reflect political, philosophical and even religious biases. There are obviously therefore, no universally accepted criteria for evaluating education, and there also appear to be no universally satisfactory criteria for evaluating careers guidance. If we attempt to derive criteria using the theories of occupational choice described in Chapter 1, we encounter immediate problems. Existing theories of occupational choice have not been adequately tested, since they tend to be largely non-predictive and so criteria based on these theories for evaluating careers guidance, are suspect.

Ultimately, it is the school-leaver who is the consumer of the Careers Advisory Service. In many other areas of life, the effectiveness of a service is judged by the degree of satisfaction of those who receive the service. Yet, in this area, the implication appears to be that the school-leavers are in some sense not capable or mature enough to judge the help they have received. More 'objective' measures are required. These 'objective' measures, however, are based upon arbitrary criteria - job changing for example, has been used as a criterion for judging the effectiveness of careers guidance. A high frequency of job changing is judged to reflect adversely upon careers guidance, whilst a low frequency is judged to be an indicator of good guidance. However, job changing can be viewed as a constructive and even necessary exercise at the beginning of working life. In order to find out where he or she is happiest, the school-leaver may need to sample a number of occupations. Similarly, concordance with guidance given - the school-leaver taking the job a careers guidance officer recommends - cannot be used as a criterion upon which to judge the effectiveness of the advice. Concordance may simply reflect conformity as a personality trait. The satisfaction of the school-leaver with the job he or she takes on the recommendation of a careers officer, may also reflect a lack of awareness of available job opportunities. Given the arbitrary nature of the criteria used for judging the effectiveness of careers guidance, clients' satisfaction would seem to be at least as good as any other. On this criterion, the careers guidance received by the school-leavers in our sample was, on the whole, unsatisfactory.

2. The Schools

Assessment of the helpfulness of schools in giving information about jobs and in finding jobs, varied considerably over time. Six months before leaving school, over 80% of the adolescents reported that the school was helpful (Table 7). However, 2½ years into working life, 60% of respondents reported that the school was unhelpful or made no difference to them (Table 8) in finding jobs.

General complaints included the need for more work experience visits and lack of detail about the requirements of different jobs. Comments included such things as:

> 'Need more people to explain about jobs, there is not enough detail'; 'too wide a scale, no specifics'; 'need more careers teaching'; 'not gone deep enough into jobs around'.

A number of children from Brookvale complained about the fact that the careers teacher tried to persuade them to take jobs they did not want, and to dissuade them from the jobs they really wanted.

The adolescents were also asked, while still at school, whether they felt that the school taught too much, the right amount, or not enough on careers. Out of 169 responses to this question, only 4% felt that the school taught too much, whereas some 41% felt that the school taught too little. There were no group differences in response to this question.

At both the initial stage and final stage of the present survey, the young people repeatedly referred to the lack of detail about specific jobs. They suggested that films, work experience and people coming to school to talk about their jobs, would provide more of this kind of detail. They also mentioned the need for more information on wages, taxes and the intricacies of pay slips, and there was an overwhelming expression of need for more information about jobs and working life generally. It would seem likely that the school is the obvious institution to meet such a need, but there was firm resistance in the schools in our survey, to any extension of time given to careers teaching. We were given the impression in both the schools we visited, that the careers teachers were fighting a lonely battle in their work, against a preponderant emphasis on the importance of exam-related subjects. We were left wondering how important a place careers lessons take in the curricula of schools, and how aware head teachers are of the important function of careers lessons in preparing young people for this transitional period.

Retrospective assessments of help received from the school in getting jobs were, on the whole, adversely critical. Only 15% of respondents reported unreservedly that the schools were helpful (Table 8). Again, these global assessments can be misleading, but the comments made by the young workers backed up their answers.

General comments were sometimes positive:

> 'Careers teacher told me of the vacancy'; 'gave me an idea of jobs to go for'; 'everyone was concerned and helpful'; 'found me my first job' 'helpful with suggestions'

but overall, the comments were preponderantly negative:

> 'Short of suggestions'; 'careers teacher was out of touch with the kind of work I wanted to do'; 'the information was out of date and there wasn't enough'; 'we weren't taught on an adult level and were not taken seriously enough'; 'only interested in the brainy ones'; 'teachers had favourites and concentrated on them'; 'we had little chance to see what jobs were like'; 'the boys were encouraged to go down the pit and the not very bright girls to go into the factory'; 'there was no effort to tell us all about different jobs'; 'only interested in above average intelligence kids'; 'careers lessons were a complete waste of time - I gained nothing from them'; 'had no time for the individual'; 'they thought we had very limited intelligence and were not capable of a responsible job'; 'if I'd listened to them I'd have ended up down the pit instead of having an apprenticeship'; 'only interested in the boys'; 'help was too general and covering too many things'; 'staff were not knowledgeable enough to advise us on the correct job for individual capabilities'.

The strength and consistency with which these opinions were expressed suggested that as far as careers lessons and careers advice within schools were concerned, the consumers were distinctly dissatisfied. It is not possible to generalise to other areas or schools, but the evidence gathered in the present survey suggests that young workers start their working lives feeling some disgruntlement at the lack, or poor quality, of teaching on careers that they received. It should be stated however, that the careers teachers in the present survey evidenced the greatest possible commitment to their work, and both were obviously personally concerned to do all they could to aid pupils to get good jobs. They undoubtedly made the most of the limited resources and time available to them.

3. Family and Friends

The influence of family and friends in the processes of occupational choice and securing employment has already been mentioned - family and friends accounted for 54% of sources mentioned in response to the question 'How did you hear about your job?' Family and friends thus appeared to be the single most important category of sources of influence and help for young people, in their transition from school to work. The answers given by the school-leavers suggested that parents were acting directly to influence their children in particular directions, and whilst some young people were being pressured into getting jobs right away (38%), a majority (62%) reported that their parents had agreed to the idea of their looking around for the right job. 69% of the young people indicated that their parents had expressed a positive wish that they should enter a particular occupation, and 74% reported that their parents had said they should not take a particular job (a good example of the latter was a job in mining).

When they were still at school the adolescents were asked what job they would like when they left school. They were then asked if they knew anyone who did this kind of work. Half of the respondents knew members of their family already doing the job they had chosen, and nearly one in four indicated that their parents were employed in this job. Altogether, 65% knew family members or friends doing the work. These figures are not altogether surprising, given that in small communities employment opportunities are limited. Some respondents were therefore likely to know family members or friends working in the occupations they had chosen. Nevertheless, the consistency of the finding that family and friends are important influences, both within and across studies, is one which merits attention. It may well be that parents should be involved more formally in the processes of careers guidance, and that official services and family influence could be integrated. Parents often have only the experiences of the jobs they have done or presently hold, but they do have the vital experience of working life which they can describe in detail to their children. Careers guidance specialists and careers teachers may often have more limited personal experience. There would certainly seem to be a case for parents to be made at least more aware of the importance of their influence, and the responsibility they therefore carry in dispensing advice.

4. Work Experience

Formal work-experience visits arranged by schools, have been shown to be effective in improving the vocational maturity of school-leavers (Pumfrey & Warm, 1972), and given the expressed need for more information on jobs in the present survey, it seems that the development of educational visits and work experience programmes should be encouraged. Hayes (1973) has shown that considerably more attention in careers teaching should be devoted to the psychosocial (interaction with others - customers, bosses, workmates; image of the organisation; product; status of the occupation) as opposed to the economic aspects of work. Educational visits would be useful in providing exactly that kind of information. However, out of the 174 school-leavers we interviewed, only 34 had been out on educational visits to factories, shops, mines etc., although 98% of all those interviewed thought that educational visits were a good idea, and were obviously keen to go on such visits. 72% of the respondents in the survey had some work experience, in the form of newspaper rounds and holiday jobs. Girls however, were less likely to have had this kind of previous experience than boys (82% of boys, as against 63% of girls). The importance of work experience in the process of vocational preparation, was therefore not reflected in the formal process of careers education, and again, it was informal learning through holiday jobs, which provided some experience of working life.

SUMMARY

By the time they left school, over half of the respondents in the present survey had secured jobs, and another one in three had found jobs within a month of leaving school. Within Woodbank school, the 'A' band pupils were much less likely to have jobs by the time they had left school than were 'B' band pupils. This latter finding was attributed to the significantly higher occupational aims of 'A' band students, which were gradually lowered to a level where they could be fulfilled. One third of the sample managed to obtain the first job for which they applied. 'A' band students made significantly more job applications than 'B' band students and this again was interpreted as reflecting their higher occupational aims.

Family and friends appeared to be the single most important source of help for young schoolleavers looking for work. Almost 40% of respondents indicated that family or friends were the sources of information about vacancies, which eventually led them to their first jobs. Less than a quarter mentioned the Careers Advisory Service as being instrumental in notifying them of vacancies which ultimately provided them with jobs, and only a third indicated that their schools or the Careers Service had provided any help at all in finding their first jobs.

Of the respondents, 30% found the Careers Advisory Service helpful and one third found the Service unhelpful or ineffective. Help received from schools in the process of finding work, and in providing information about work, was generally criticised. 60% of respondents reported retrospectively (2½ years after leaving school) that the school was either unhelpful or made no difference to them in their search for jobs. Lack of detailed information about jobs was the criticism most frequently directed at careers teaching in schools.

Finally, the influence of family and friends in securing work for the youngsters was paramount, and it is suggested that the importance of the influence of parents be recognised and utilized. 'Work experience' and educational visits were also seen by respondents as important sources of information and they are undoubtedly useful in providing important information about psycho-social aspects of work.

As consumers of Careers Advisory Services and careers lessons, the respondents in the present survey appeared to be dissatisfied with the information and help they received. Most had jobs within a short time of leaving school however, and it therefore seems likely that the source of dissatisfaction was not related to the problems of finding work per se. It is more likely that their dissatisfaction was a result of some other factor. One possibility, which is explored in Chapter 5, is that there was a lack of concordance between the jobs they had aimed at while they were at school and their ultimate attainments.

Chapter Five

AIMS AND ATTAINMENTS

Occupational choices voiced by adolescents just before they leave school represent, in part, their hopes for their future lives. These choices or occupational aims may or may not be fulfilled, and attainment or non-attainment can therefore have far-reaching effects upon the individual's life. We are still largely ignorant however, of why it is that some school-leavers achieve their aims and some do not, and this gap in our knowledge is an obstacle to effective careers guidance and careers teaching. Inevitably, we are reliant on occupational choice theorists for explanations of why some school-leavers achieve occupational aims and why some do not. The differentialists emphasise factors such as the abilities, interests and dislikes of youngsters leaving school, and the extent to which these match the characteristics of jobs already existing in the labour market, as important in predicting which individuals will achieve their occupational aims. The developmentalists on the other hand, would see the vocational maturity of the individual, his or her awareness of the world of work, and knowledge of the local labour market, as vital. Those who advocate approaches which emphasise social forces rather than the attributes of the individual, such as Roberts (1975), might stress 'climates of expectation' associated with particular educational institutions. Thus, they would predict that aspirations would be moulded by the 'hidden curriculum' within schools, so that the less academically able would have much lower aspirations. Others (e.g. Carter, 1962) have described how local employment patterns will limit the type of employment available to school leavers and therefore, the extent to which their aims can be met. National and international economic changes will also affect the relationship between occupational choices and attainments, as will a large variety of variables(e.g. a decline in the birth rate affects the demand for teachers where a government is not committed to reducing classroom sizes, so opportunities for prospective teachers would be limited).

What has research shown about the usefulness of each of these approaches, in predicting the match between occupational aims and attainments? Is it true for example,that individual schools exert a strong influence? Are there differences between boys and girls, in their success in achieving the aims they articulated at school? How important is careers teaching in the school, in influencing the concordance between occupational aims and attainments? Surprisingly, very few studies have examined in any detail the relationship between occupational aims, stated just prior to school-leaving, and ultimate attainments. Carter (1962) interviewed 200 school-leavers early in their last term at school, again at three months after they had left school, and finally one year into working life. He found that one-third of the boys and just under half of the girls took jobs which were the same or very similar to those they had chosen in the school interview. In Veness' (1962) study, just under one-third of the boys and over half of the girls fulfilled their occupational aspirations. These findings suggest that it is boys rather than girls who experience frustration of their aims upon beginning working life. However, this conclusion is contradicted by the results of a questionnaire survey of young workers who had left school within the previous three years (Maizels, 1970). The young workers were asked how different were the jobs they had obtained, from the jobs they had originally wanted. Just under 40% of the boys and over one-third of the girls indicated that jobs wanted and obtained were more or less identical.

All of these studies were carried out during times of relatively low unemployment (between 1951 and 1956) and no recent study has examined the relationship between aims and attainments in the high unemployment of the 1970s. Furthermore, statistical testing of results has been lacking in these surveys and while they have served admirably to provide a rough picture of the relationship between aims and attainments, no attempts have been made to discover what factors are significantly associated with adolescents fulfilling their occupational aims.

Maizels (1970) examined the relationships between aims and attainments and social class background, position in stream, age at leaving school, and sources of help in deciding on and obtaining employment. She found a closer correspondence between the aims and attainments of the sons of manual workers, than was the case for the sons of non-manual workers; that leavers from the higher ability streams had to modify their original aims more often than those from lower ability streams; and finally, that boys who relied on their parents for advice and girls who came to their decisions without help, more often fulfilled their occupational aims than others. These findings, however, were based only on apparent trends and no results of statistical significance testing are reported. Thus, Maizels' findings can at best be regarded as only indicative that methods adopted, type of help sought, and type of help received in the process of job choice, are associated with the attainment of vocational aims. This research provides a picture of the variations in the correspondence between aims and attainments in different locations at different times. But what evidence does it provide in favour of the various theories of occupational choice? The answer is, unfortunately, very little, and this is partially because various researchers have not set out with the idea of examining the usefulness of different approaches. Rather, they have traced patterns of experience of young people in the transition from school to work, and their results have provided tantalising clues about the various factors influencing the transition. In the present survey, we examined aims and attainments in the hope that some factors associated with vocational success (measured by the correspondence between aims and attainments) could be discovered. We also hoped to uncover evidence in favour of the various theories of occupational choice which attempt to explain and predict how choices are made.

RESULTS

1. Occupational Attainments
Six months prior to leaving school and entering the new world of work, the young people voiced a particular occupational choice. Nine months later, and again two and a half years after they had left school, they were contacted and asked to provide information about the jobs they currently held. The

aims they had expressed at school could thus be compared with their attainments at these times.

Occupational aims at school and occupational attainments at 2½ years into working life are shown in Table 1. Among the boys the most popular choices were apprenticeships, mining, forces and engineering, while the girls chose office work, machining (in the textile industry) and shopwork most frequently. There proved to be a highly significant relationship between total number of examination passes at CSE and GCE level, and the socio-economic status of the jobs attained. School-leavers with most examination passes tended to be given jobs of higher socio-economic status. Many fewer boys actually secured apprenticeships than had originally wanted them, and proportionately more of the school-leavers were doing some kind of office work (clerk, secretary, receptionist etc.) than had originally wished for this kind of work.

Job aims most unlikely to be fulfilled were teaching, nursery nursing and engineering. Overall, the degree of correspondence between jobs aimed at and jobs obtained was 49.6%- 68 out of the 137 young people contacted at 2½ years into working life, had achieved their occupational aims. There were no significant differences between bands or sexes in the degree of correspondence between aims and attainments (Table 2). In other word, male school-leavers were as likely to attain their aims as were female school-leavers; 'B' band pupils similarly were as likely to get the jobs they wanted as were 'A' band pupils. Pupils from Woodbank (the banded school) were less likely to achieve their aims than Brookvale pupils (Woodbank - 41.2%; Brookvale - 58% achieved aims), though this finding did not reach statistical significance (Table 2). This latter difference between the schools is of some interest, since it may reflect the fact that pupils from Woodbank originally set their occupational aims higher than the Brookvale pupils (Chapter 3). It may be that Woodbank pupils had more difficulty in getting the jobs they aimed at, because their initial aims were high.

There were no differences between sexes or between schools in the socio-economic status of the jobs obtained. Pupils from Brookvale school were as likely to get jobs of high status, as Woodbank students. Similarly, boys and girls did not differ in the status of the jobs they obtained. Within Woodbank school, 'A' band pupils, on average, secured jobs of significantly higher status than

TABLE 1

OCCUPATION	AIMS No. OF RESPONDENTS (6 months prior to school leaving)	%	ATTAINMENTS No. OF RESPONDENTS (2½ years after school leaving)	%
Apprenticeships	31	17.8	19	13.9
Office work	25	14.4	27	19.7
Machinist (textile industry)	17	9.8	23	16.8
Mining	15	8.6	14	10.2
Forces	11	6.3	11	8.0
Teaching	11	6.3	0	0.0
Shop work	8	4.6	8	5.8
Nursery Nurse	7	4.0	1	0.7
Engineering	7	4.0	1	0.7
Police	4	2.3	0	0.0
Nursing	4	2.3	1	0.7
Technician/Science Research	3	1.7	2	1.5
Business	3	1.7	3	2.2
Draughtsman	3	1.7	2	1.5
Cookery	2	1.2	2	1.5
Driver	2	1.2	0	0.0
Solicitor	2	1.2	0	0.0
Hairdresser	2	1.2	3	2.2
Embroiderer	2	1.2	0	0.0
Bank clerk	0	0.0	4	2.9
Others (e.g. economist, journalist, pilot, footballer)	11	6.2	16	11.7
Don't know	4	2.3	–	–
N =	174	100	137	100

jobs obtained by 'B' band students. This is consistent with both the fact that 'A' band pupils had more examination passes on average, when they left school, and with our finding that those with more examination passes tended to get jobs of higher status (such as laboratory technician, insurance underwriter, assistant librarian, bank clerk etc.).It is also consistent with the higher occupational aims set by 'A' band pupils for themselves while they were still at school.

2. Status of Job Aims and Attainments

It was possible to examine the relationship between jobs aimed at and jobs obtained in more detail than simply looking at correspondence between aims and attainments. By examining the relationship between socio-economic status of jobs aimed at and the status of the jobs attained, we were able to assess whether the respondents were aiming high and modifying their aims, or whether their aims proved to be realistic. So, if there was no difference between the status of the jobs aimed at and the status of the jobs actually obtained by the school-leavers, we could assume that their aims were realistic. However, if there proved to be a difference between status of aims and attainments, with status of aims being higher than status of attainmnents(e.g.wanting a job as an infants' teacher and ending up as a shelf-filler in a supermarket),then there would be more basis for assuming that the initial aims of the school-leavers were unrealistically high.

Overall, there was no difference between the socio-economic status of jobs aimed at and jobs attained, suggesting that the adolescents in our sample were realistic in their aims. Similarly, there were no differences in status of jobs aimed at and obtained between sexes, bands, or those with high numbers of exam passes and those with low numbers or no exam passes. However, students from Woodbank school obtained jobs of significantly lower status than they had originally hoped for. They appeared therefore to be moderating their original aims in order to secure employment. The same was not true of pupils from Brookvale school (Table 3). This finding cannot be explained by differences between pupils in the two schools in their academic ability since the ability of pupils in the two schools was similar. Furthermore, the difference was not confined to one of the bands in Woodbank. Whilst pupils from Brookvale school obtained jobs, on average, of higher status

TABLE 2   Correspondence between jobs aimed at and jobs attained

	% obtaining jobs aimed at	% failing to obtain jobs aimed at	N
Total	49.6	50.4	137
Woodbank School	41.2	58.8	68
Brookvale School	58.0	42.0	69
Males	48.5	51.5	68
Females	52.2	47.8	69
'A' band) − Woodbank	37.8	62.2	37
'B' band)	45.2	54.8	31

TABLE 3   Status of jobs aimed at and obtained by pupils from Woodbank and Brookvale schools

		WOODBANK SCHOOL		BROOKVALE SCHOOL	
Socio-economic status of job		Aims	Attainments	Aims	Attainments
High	1	5	8	1	3
	2	26	2	7	6
	3	27	27	33	24
	4	17	23	30	28
Low	5	11	9	12	5

83

(though non-significantly) than they had aimed for, pupils from both the 'A' and 'B' bands of Woodbank took jobs of lower status than those at which they had aimed.

Having discovered which students fulfilled their occupational aims it was possible to investigate whether patterns of choice differed between those who attain their aims and those who do not. Socio-economic status of jobs aimed at proved to be significantly higher amongst those who did not achieve their aims. Thus, aiming for higher status jobs whilst still at school appeared to be a predictor of the likelikhood of not obtaining occupational aims. It remained a possibility that those who found the jobs they had originally hoped for, might have done so only by virtue of the fact that their original aims were low, and that those who did not attain their aims, nevertheless obtained jobs of signigicantly higher status because their aims had originally been high. If this were true, it could be argued that by aiming high, adolescents would get better jobs, even though they would be less likely to obtain the particular jobs at which they were aiming. This did not prove to be the case. There were no significant differences in status of jobs obtained between those attaining original aims and those not.

DISCUSSION

Overall therefore, respondents in the present survey were more likely to get the jobs aimed at than respondents in previous surveys. This may be due to the difference in unemployment levels (5.5% in the survey area and 6.0% nationally at the time our survey was conducted) and the lower unemployment levels nationally and locally at the times previous studies were carried out (between 1951 and 1965). It is possible that the young people in our sample, aware of the restricted number of job opportunities nationally, and the problems of getting jobs which were being widely publicised at the time, were much more willing to temper their aims initially, and to set goals for themselves which might be more easily reached. Alternatively, of course, a variety of other variables might have been responsible. For example, some of the adolescents in our sample expressed a dislike of travelling away to work, and many may therefore have set themselves aims which they knew they could probably achieve locally. It seems likely, however, that adolescents would modify their occupational aims with changes in the economic climate, and this possibility might usefully be examined in more detail.

'A' band pupils within Woodbank school secured jobs of higher status than the pupils of 'B' band and this reflects both their higher aims and the fact that they left school with better qualifications. However, the pupils from Woodbank were less likely (though not significantly so) to achieve their occupational aims than the students of Brookvale, and were more likely to obtain jobs of lower status than those at which they had originally aimed. Furthermore, the status of the jobs they attained was not significantly different from the status of jobs attained by the children of Brookvale school. Finally, socio-economic status of jobs aimed at was significantly higher amongst those who did not attain their aims. This suggests that the pupils of Brookvale set themselves 'realistic' aims which they were able to fulfill. Indeed, these pupils did have significantly lower occupational aims than those of Woodbank (see Chapter 3). It suggests also, therefore, that the Woodbank pupils set themselves unrealistically high targets which had to be modified. It also proved not to be the case that by aiming high, regardless of ability, adolescents obtained better jobs. These findings are consistent with the notion that beginning workers cannot usually enter the occupational hierarchy at levels higher than those merited by their educational achievements (Crowther Report, 1959).

The differences between the pupils in the two schools, in the correspondence between aims and attainments, cannot be explained by differences between catchment areas, numbers of pupils, or differences in levels of ability. There were no major differences on any of these variables when the two schools were compared. Two possible explanations suggest themselves. The first is that the different systems of school organization - banding in Woodbank, mixed-ability teaching in Brookvale- had some effect upon pupils' occupational aims. This explanation however, has to take into account the fact that aims were raised amongst both 'A' and 'B' band pupils. This would argue somewhat against the idea that banding systems and stratified education systems produce 'climates of expectation' associated with the individual's place in the system. If that were the case, we would have expected 'B' band pupils not to have to lower their aims in order to get jobs, since their aims would already have been depressed, as a result of their labelling as 'educational failures'. In fact, both 'A' and 'B' band pupils in Woodbank had to lower their aims, before they were able to secure employment. Nevertheless, it may be that the system of banding did influence overall levels of expectation in Woodbank school. It is possible that 'B' band students were influenced by the higher expectations of the 'A'band pupils. There may have been a 'slipstream effect' in which the aims of the 'B' band pupils were pulled upwards by the high aims of the 'A' band pupils, even though there were overall differences between the bands. Alternatively, as we have argued previously, 'B' band pupils may not have been content to be labelled as failures in the world of work. Having experienced that label in school, they may have been more determined to succeed, and so aimed at jobs of relatively high status in the labour market.

A second explanation is that the careers teaching at the two schools was responsible for the differences in aims and attainments described above. The careers teaching in Woodbank school was based on the developmental approaches to occupational guidance, elaborated by Ginzberg et al (1951) and Super (1957). The careers teacher at Brookvale, however, employed techniques prompted by the differentialist or matching model. Roberts (1975) has criticised the developmental approach because he says, contrary to the theory of developmentalists, individuals do not choose the job they obtain; they simply take what is available. Thus, Roberts proposes that one needs information concerning the educational qualifications and the local job opportunity structure, and not the aspirations of the school-leaver, in order to predict the type of job a school-leaver will take. He argues further that the developmental theory of occupational choice is only pertinent to those educationally more able youngsters who are able to make genuine career decisions. Indeed, Ginzberg's research was initially carried out using subjects who were graduates from high schools and who went to college. Roberts goes on to argue that

> 'No amount of guidance, whatever its character, will change the realities of work in an industrial society. Discussing guidance as if it could hope to extend to all individuals the opportunities for self-actualization at work

currently available for only a few and widen the horizons of individuals whose scope for occupation choice is limited, merely obscures the reality of the situation.......... the principal consequence will simply be that careers guidance will aggravate rather than resolve individuals' difficulties in adjusting to the opportunity structures that confront them.' (Roberts, 1975)

Our findings would therefore appear to support these arguments. Those who were taught along developmental lines in careers lessons (Woodbank school-leavers) did appear to widen their horizons to jobs of higher status. When actually confronted with the local job opportunity structure, they had to make a greater adjustment than the Brookvale students whose aims appeared to have been 'realistic' prior to leaving school. However, this cannot be seen as a simple argument against encouraging school-leavers to aim for the best jobs they could possibly get. In some cases such encouragement may end ultimately in frustration and disappointment. For example, Susan D. in our sample, had wanted and had been encouraged to get a job as a nursery nurse, but despite repeated applications and enquiries, eventually had to accept a job as a machinist in a local textile factory. At the same time, there is every possibility that some may obtain better jobs than they hoped for. Shirley J. who had hoped to get a job with a large manufacturing organization as a senior secretary, was eventually appointed as an export liaison officer. Similarly, Daniel E. who had hoped to be a professional footballer, was encouraged by family and friends, and is now playing football for a club in the first division of the English League. Nevertheless, because there were no differences overall in status of jobs attained between those who achieved and those who did not achieve their occupational aims, we are forced to conclude that, by aiming high, adolescents do not on the average get better jobs.

These two explanations (academic organization and careers teaching) are not, of course, mutually exclusive nor comprehensive, and other explanations of our findings are also possible. It may be, for example, that the young people in our survey took the first job they were offered, simply because they were worried about not getting any other, and that subsequent jobs were dictated by the opportunity structures in employment through which they passed.

The reasons given by young people for taking the jobs they held and for accepting work different from their original aims are therefore of some interest.

REASONS FOR ACCEPTING JOBS

In the studies conducted in the area of transition from school to work, very little attention has been paid to the reasons given by young workers for taking particular jobs. The problems of accepting reasons given at their face value have been discussed earlier. However, accepting with caution the evidence given by the young workers themselves, would seem to be a necessary preliminary to a detailed examination of this area.

Maizels (1970) asked the young people in her study why they had relinquished their original job aims and found that the main reasons offered by boys was lack of necessary qualifications. The girls on the other hand reportedly took up alternative employment because they believed working conditions were better elsewhere.

In the present survey, those young workers who were not doing the jobs they had originally aimed at were asked, at nine months after leaving school, how they felt about having decided to do a different job. Their responses are shown in Table 4. While nearly 50% stated that they were not bothered, a further 37% indicated that they were either sorry or still looking for jobs of their original choice. Such a finding argues somewhat against the ideas that young workers are satisfied with the kinds of work they enter and that they experience the transition from school to work as relatively smooth (Ashton, 1973). The young workers were also asked what had made them change their minds about the job they had wanted to do. The answers were overwhelmingly biased in the direction of forced choice. None of those who responded to this question, indicated a better alternative as the reason for taking a different job. By far the most frequently mentioned reason for the change of mind was the lack of vacancies (41.9% of responses):

> 'Not many jobs available'; 'I was fed up with looking and there were not many jobs about'; 'no vacancies in the RAF'; 'I couldn't get the job I wanted so I just had to take this one'; 'no jobs available at the time'; 'I just couldn't get shop work'; 'there were no vacancies at the pottery'; 'this was the only one

available'; 'no vacancies with the GPO'.

Other reasons included lack of qualifications:

> 'It's the only thing open unless you got 'A' levels'; 'I wasn't old enough and didn't want to move away from home'; 'you can't be a fireman until you're 18'; 'I couldn't get on a nursing course'; 'I would have to take exams to be a hairdresser'.

Only two of the 43 people who answered this question mention wages as a factor in their change of minds. Nearly one in four of those who were doing jobs different from their original aims indicated that desperation was the reason for their decision to take a different job. This is another indication that the process of transition is perhaps not quite as smooth as has been claimed by researchers in the past.

At this time (nine months into working life) all the young workers were asked what things had made them decide to take the particular job they were now doing. Some gave a number of reasons e.g. 'near home, wages quite good and it's clean work', where others gave only one e.g. 'didn't want to go on the dole'. All the responses were given equal weighting and the breakdown of these responses in categories is shown in Table 5. By far the most frequently given reason was the non-availability of jobs:

> 'I didn't want to be unemployed'; 'there were no other vacancies available' 'it's better than being on the dole'; 'there's just not anything available'; 'I couldn't find anything else'; 'not many jobs about'; 'I didn't think there was much possibility of getting another job'; 'it was a case of having to take a job'; 'jobs were scarce so I took the first job I was offered'; 'I was out of work'; 'I was frightened of not getting a job'.

Out of 100 respondents to this question 30 gave reasons such as these for accepting their jobs. In our survey, therefore, nearly a third took jobs for negative reasons (i.e. because they couldn't get other jobs or were worried about unemployment). Such a finding suggests that the relevance of developmental theories of careers choices is somewhat restricted, at least in the case of a large proportion of less qualified young workers.

A smaller percentage of responses was related to the conditions and intrinsic satisfactions of jobs, e.g.

> 'It's a clean job';'it sounded interesting from what my sister said'; 'it's respectable'; 'I thought it was good fun, easy going and there were friendly people'; 'there is a friendly atmosphere'; 'it's interesting and varied'.

TABLE 4   School-leavers' attitudes to their having to take jobs which were different from those at which they originally aimed

CATEGORY	% OF RESPONDENTS
Still looking	22.2
Very sorry	2.2
Somewhat sorry	13.3
Not bothered	48.9
Somewhat pleased	6.7
Quite pleased	6.7
N =	45

TABLE 5   School-leavers' reasons for accepting the jobs they were doing

REASONS	% OF RESPONDENTS
No other jobs available	30
Conditions good (good atmosphere or interesting work)	16
Money	13
It was the job wanted	12
Near home	10
Good prospects	8
Advised by parents or friends	5
Good training	4
Other	2
N =	100

Money and good wages accounted for 13% of the total number of responses and nearly 10% of responses were to do with the proximity of the work to the respondents' homes.

It is apparent therefore that reasons given for taking jobs, are very different from those given for choosing jobs (see Chapter 3), and that the respondents in the present survey had little choice in deciding on their occupations. This finding argues strongly against basing careers guidance on theories of occupational choice. There is no doubt that in some cases careers guidance has the effect of restricting the range of jobs an individual is likely to envisage taking, but, given the lack of correspondence in many cases between aims and attainments, there would seem to be a case for basing guidance as much on patterns of job attainments in local areas as on job aims of schoolleavers. Thus, individuals who choose jobs for which there are few vacancies available, will need to be made aware of that fact, if their transition from school to work is to be made smoother. It would seem logical that those who expect difficulties will tend on the whole to cope with them better than those who do not.

The picture painted by respondents in their reasons for taking jobs is, as a whole, somewhat gloomy. If 30% of youngsters nationally took jobs 'because I didn't want to go on the dole', it suggests that concepts such as 'implementing mature self concepts' in working life are irrelevant to the experience of many young people in the country at this time. Whilst it is unwise to generalise from one small area to the whole of the country, it is disquieting that for so many in our sample, where work was more readily available than elsewhere in the country, the entry into work was not that originally envisaged and hoped for. It suggests that developmental and even differentialist approaches to occupational choice are very limited by existing social and economic climates.

The picture is not totally gloomy, however. Nearly one in four of the respondents took jobs because the conditions, training or prospects were good, or because it was the job they had originally wanted. It is also of some interest that 10% of reasons given for taking jobs fell in the category 'near to home'. It would be useful to compare different communities and sub-groups to discover the relevance of this item. It might well be, for example, that those living in cities would be more geographically mobile in employment terms than those living in mining villages, and the relevance of social factors such as these to careers guidance might then be discovered and applied. For example, there are areas of Britain, such as the South East, where jobs are more readily available, while some areas have been badly hit by unemployment in recent years e.g. Glasgow, South Wales. It is becoming increasingly apparent that, if school-leavers in areas of high unemployment are to get work, they must be prepared to move away or at least be more mobile. There are obvious difficulties in trying to separate out the relevance of such social factors to careers guidance, but it is certainly true that, given existing economic and social conditions, it is these factors which need to be investigated if the useful application of theories is to be achieved.

SUMMARY

The relationship between occupational aims and attainments was examined and half of the young people in our sample were found to be working in jobs they had aimed for while they were at school. Particular job aims such as teaching, nursery nursing and engineering, were less likely to be fulfilled than others.

Those from Woodbank (the banded school) secured jobs of significantly lower status than they had originally hoped for. The same was not true of Brookvale school and there were no differences between the two schools in status of jobs acquired. This result could well be explained by the differences between the two schools in academic organization, but another explanation is that the different styles of careers teaching adopted in the two schools (developmental in Woodbank and differentialist in Brookvale) were responsible. These findings are also seen as offering some support for Roberts' (1975) proposals that the developmental approach will aggravate rather than ease difficulties in adjusting to the opportunity structures of work.

Socio-economic status of jobs aimed at proved to be significantly higher amongst those who did not achieve their aims. There were no differences in status of jobs attained between those who achieved, and those who did not achieve their occupational aims. It is concluded that by aiming high adolescents did not necessarily get better jobs. If we wish to be in a position to advise, then more research needs to be carried out to examine the relationship between aims and attainments and the psychological effect of failure to attain aims.

In an examination of reasons given for accepting jobs, it was found that lack of suitable vacancies and fear of unemployment were seen as important by some 40% of respondents. The differences between occupational choice and occupational attainments, and the differences between the reasons given by young people for both, were found to be substantial. When choosing jobs the school-leavers generally gave reasons which were couched in positive terms e.g. 'I like working with children'; 'It's a good job with plenty of security'; 'It pays well and the people are friendly'. But when it came to taking jobs, a depressingly negative picture is painted by young people at the outset of their working lives: 'It is better than being on the dole'; 'there wasn't anything else available'; 'I was frightened of not getting a job'. That their view of their working lives should change so quickly, from one of hopeful enthusiasm to one of depressed resignation, is some indication of how ill-prepared they were for this new life. It should be apparent that basing careers guidance and careers teaching on theories of occupational choice, has little value in today's economic world - at least for the majority of school-leavers. It would surely be better if careers teaching were based as much upon patterns of occupational attainments in local areas and amongst local sub-groups, as on theories of occupational choice, which have less and less relevance to the realities of the world of work in a time of economic recession.

Chapter Six

ENTRY INTO WORK

> 'I walked in on the Monday morning and I was really frightened. I'd not realised how many there'd be - there were so many of them, all staring. At least I thought they were. Then, all morning I was really ... ham-fisted, I didn't know where things were or what to do. It was like being a little kid again'.

This account of the experience of Sheila, one of the school-leavers in our sample, is similar to what most of us feel when we start a new job. For the school-leaver however, the feelings of apprehension and helplessness are probably far greater than they are for the worker changing jobs in the middle of his or her working life. The young school-leaver, after a life of dependence at home, is being asked to assume independence; after a school-life of discipline and being told what to do, the school-leaver is faced with the prospect of the responsibility of the role of adult worker. After a period of training the fifth form boy may have to take responsibility for signalling the starts and stops on dangerous conveyor belt systems underground; the girl who is given a traditional female job such as hair-dressing, may worry about putting soap in a customer's eyes or burning a customer's head with over-hot water. But the first days of working life are not only important because they fill the young worker with trepidation - they also serve to confirm and deny initial hopes and expectations. In many ways they are a foundation of experience, which will underlie future perceptions of the world of work as well as interpretations of subsequent experiences. And it is for this latter reason that the entry of the school-leaver into work is a crucial process, since the first impressions of,for example, management or trade unions, may be impressions which linger throughout working life. For the adult worker, a change of job is less crucial, since many aspects of working life will remain the same. The adult worker will also be better preared to deal with the new experiences in working life, by relating them to past experiences, and to observations of others' experiences. For the school-leaver, entry into full-time employment will often mark the first direct experience of the world of work, with its multiplicity of formal and informal rules, codes of practice and norms. The adolescent will have to learn many of these for the first time, and so the socialization to work of the school-leaver is likely to be a longer, more intensive and probably more traumatic process.

Yet, to the adolescent, keen to leave school and assume the role of adult in our society, the first days at work are anticipated with impatience. The vast majority in our survey were eagerly awaiting their release from school, and their start in working life. It was almost as though most of the latter years of their school lives had been endured on the basis of the promise that their future lives held. Some hint of how working life measured up to the expectations of the adolescents was given in their reasons for accepting jobs. Surprisingly perhaps, it is only hints that we have about the entry to work of young people. As in a number of fields in the area of transition from school to work, research on the entry of young people into their first full-time work is sparse and limited to a very few field studies.

PREVIOUS RESEARCH INTO THE ENTRY TO WORK

Carter's (1962) study in Sheffield concentrated less on quantitative analysis of the process of transition from school to work, and more on qualitative descriptions of the subjective experiences of the young people in the study. These descriptions are rich with evocative accounts of the nervousness and excitement felt by adolescents beginning their working lives. Carter reports that boys and girls worried about things such as whether they would report to the wrong entrance of the factory, and about whether they would be able to do the work without making mistakes. Some were calmed by employers who told them not to worry, but others were placed at assembly lines and had to keep up with machines and conveyors right from the start. From the results of this study, it appeared that adolescents were very anxious about meeting new people and about going through 'the gradual process of getting accepted, before, suddenly, you find you are one of them'. One girl commented 'I was so shy I could hardly speak and so nervous I could not eat my dinner'. However, Carter reports that the excitement and nervousness gradually wore off 'when machines had lost their magic, overalls had become commonplace, lipstick a habit, and work a bore'.

Many of the adolescents interviewed in this survey had only a vague idea of what to expect of their jobs and of work, and most were surprised and even astonished at various aspects. Carter comments on the finding that many adolescents were impressed by the free atmosphere at work, where people could 'walk about and talk, and chew and sing and smoke'. Some adolescents in the study were surprised at the mundanity of jobs they were given, whilst others were pleased by the important tasks they were asked to undertake. The over-riding impression created was that many aspects of working life were suprising to the adolescents (whether pleasantly or unpleasantly), and these were generally aspects which were not alluded to in careers talks and induction programmes.

Indeed, Carter found that only a small minority of firms at which the respondents worked, had formal induction schemes anyway, and that even where they existed, their impact appeared negligible. He reported that most young people were given only a minimum of information about work by those in charge, and were not shown around the firm. Basic information, such as where the canteen was located or how long breaks lasted, was omitted and the adolescents were understandably reluctant to ask questions continually. Informal help from co-workers was reportedly of considerable importance in the socialization process, and it appeared that other workers did much to ease the way for the young workers. The latter were surprised that other people were helpful, kind and 'right sociable'. This was not true in all cases however, and hostility was occasionally apparent (due sometimes to the individual being appointed to a better job than co-workers, or unfavourable comparisons with the person whom the young worker was replacing).

In Maizels' (1970) study, more attention was paid to the number of respondents replying in particular ways and, as a result, overall trends of experiences of youngsters entering work are estimated, though the richness of descriptions of subjective experience, characteristic of Carter's study, tends to be lost. Maizels found that over half of the 330 youngsters in her sample were shown how to do their jobs by a fellow worker. One in three of the girls and one in four of the boys referred to a supervisor as the person who demonstrated the work for them. Training instructors were mentioned by less than one in ten of the young workers, and almost all of the instructors were employed by larger firms (500 or more employees). Most of the young workers had not been trained for their jobs prior to starting the work; they were more likely to have to learn the job by actually doing it in the work setting. In addition to the training they received at work over half the boys, but less than one fifth of the girls, were attending vocational classes. There was an apparent relationship between level of skill and length of training. Average total training times (to learn the job) were estimated by boys at 7 to 10 months, and by girls at 4 to 6 months.

In a recent study of transition from school to work (Paul, 1979), 244 young workers were asked about their introductions to their firms. For 25% of the sample, more than a day was spent introducing them to the firm and the work, but for almost half, less than an hour was spent on these introductions. For 15% no introductions were made. One third of all the respondents reported that they were not trained for any period, and half of these were girls in office and shop jobs. Of all respondents, about 10% reported that 'no-one in particular' showed them how to do their jobs; 39% reported that 'a fellow worker' showed them; 28% reported that a supervisor or senior manager was responsible, and 23% mentioned training instructors.

Keil (1977), in a careful and thorough research study, examined the social processes involved in introducing young people to work, and their induction into full-time employment. Young people were interviewed in a number of different organizations in varying employment sectors e.g. public sector - Central Government, Nationalised Industries etc. The findings of this survey suggested that young people have a wide range of knowledge about their work situations; that members of management work on the assumption that young people do no have a thorough knowledge of work before entering employment, and that management attempts to structure the ways in which information reaches their new employees; that 70% of young workers were told everything they wanted to know on their induction into work; and that overall, there appeared to be satisfaction amongst managers and young workers alike with existing induction practices. The rosy picture of socialization to work may not, however, be a true reflection of the process undergone by most young workers. Keil's survey involved firms which were large in terms of number of people employed. Certainly, larger firms would be more likely to have formal induction programmes than smaller firms and would be more likely to employ Personnel Managers. Secondly, much of the information on induction practices was gleaned from interviews with management themselves, who would be more likely to present a positive picture of their induction practices than an adversely critical picture. Thirdly, and perhaps crucially, the young people in the work organizations who provided information about work induction practices, were chosen 'in consultation with the management'. There is certainly a possibility that management would select - whether consciously or unconsciously - individuals known to conform or to be non-critical of management practices, in order to present a good public image. This possible bias, in the design of the study, may therefore have affected the results to produce a picture of induction to work as a well-organized and relatively smooth process.

As far as we are aware, these are the only studies conducted in Britain which have centred on the initial entry of school-leavers into working life. Other work, conducted in the general areas of transition from school to work and organizational entry, has some relevance however. Wanous (1977), in a review of the literature on organizational entry, concluded that the expectations held by an individual of an organization he or she is considering joining, are almost always inflated. This does not apply however to those expectations that are 'concrete' e.g. pay and working hours. Wanous also found that, of the four studies which have examined changes in attitudes to organizations over the time since induction (Bray et al, 1974; Lawler et al, 1975; Vroom and Deci, 1971; Wanous, 1975), all showed that increasing experience in a new organization is associated with a less favourable view of it. Expectations of the future, and favourable perceptions of the present, appear to decrease for most newcomers to an organization for at least one year and, in one study (Bray et al, 1974), the drop continued for 6 years. The use of realistic job previews however, is reported to consistently reduce the turnover of newcomers for a wide variety of organizations (Weitz, 1957; Wanous, 1977).

One way that realistic job previews can be given to adolescents is through the formal provision of periods of work experience, in individual fields of interest, prior to their leaving school. In an examination of the school-release work experience programmes in three areas of Britain, Youthaid(1979) found that provision ranged for such programmes between none at all and provision for 50% of pupils. When young people were asked how schools should prepare them for working life, work experience was the most frequently suggested method. Perhaps significantly, the more work experience a school offered, the more likely its pupils were to say that their last year at school was a good preparation for working life. As the authors of the report go on to point out, this was one of the few areas of the curriculum where pupils were asking for more education rather than less.

It was not within the scope of the present survey to undertake a detailed study of all the processes involved in school-leavers' entry to work. Instead, it was decided to focus on two aspects of this socialization process: (1) the formal structured process of occupational socialization (training procedures, job demonstrations etc.), and (2) the formal organizational socialization (formal introductions to the firm and the work). An attempt was also made to discover the outstanding characteristics of the initial stages of the socialization to work process, as perceived by the young people themselves.

RESULTS

1. Attitudes to Training

Before leaving school the adolescents were asked whether they would be willing to undertake training for a job, and there was an overwhelmingly positive response to this question. Out of 174 respondents, all but two indicated that they would be willing to train. The enthusiasm and willingness of these young people for work can be judged also by the fact that over 50% were willing to train for longer than five years for a job, if this was necessary (Table 1). These figures are some indication of how committed the majority of the school-leavers in our sample were to the idea of investing their time and energy in the pursuit of their careers. The impression is given by the school-leavers of being keen to leave school in order to start work, not just to leave behind the discipline and boredom of school life. Indeed, the interviewers, during the school interviews, were consistently struck by the optimistic enthusiasm of school-leavers contemplating their working lives.

Within Woodbank school, there was a significant difference between the 'A' band and 'B' band pupils in the length of time for which they were willing to train. 'B' band pupils appeared to be less willing to train for long periods than 'A' band pupils. This finding may be interpreted in the light of Woodbank pupils' school experiences. It has been suggested elsewhere (Chapter 1) that the 'B' band students were likely to form a sub-culture within the school, tending to reject the formal organizational values, including formal education itself. It may be that this attitude to formal education carried over in small measure to their attitudes to training. The 'B' band students were reinforced during their school lives to believe in themselves as educationally less able and less successful, and their relative reluctance to undertake long periods of training might well derive from a lack of belief in their ability to succeed in an educational setting. Such an interpretation is supported by our finding that there was no significant relationship between exam passes overall and length of time for which respondents were willing to train. Similarly, there were no significant differences between 'A' band pupils and Brookvale pupils in the length of time for which they were willing to train, nor between 'B' band pupils and Brookvale pupils. These findings suggest therefore that the organization of Woodbank into streams, had the effect of polarising attitudes to education and formal training. The possibility that such a system can affect pupils' willingness to undertake training for work is a serious one, which neither educationalists nor employers can afford to overlook.

2. Training Received
On beginning work the school-leavers in our sample were unlikely to receive any set length of course instruction (Table 2). Only 35% of those entering work were given apprenticeships or set training courses. Of the remainder, almost all (47.7% of the whole sample) received only informal training, for example from a fellow worker, and the rest -

TABLE 1 Length of time for which school-leavers were willing to train for a job

LENGTH OF TIME	% OF RESPONDENTS
Less than 6 months	6.8
6 to 12 months	10.7
1 to 2 years	14.6
2 to 3 years	16.5
More than 5 years	51.5

TABLE 2 Type of training received by young people entering work

TYPE OF TRAINING	NUMBER OF RESPONDENTS	%	MALES	%	FEMALES	%
Apprenticeship	21	24.4	19	50.0	2	4.1
Formal (Set length and course of instruction)	9	10.5	4	10.5	5	10.4
Informal	41	47.7	8	21.1	33	68.8
No training	15	17.4	7	18.4	8	16.7
N =	86	100	38	100	48	100

nearly one fifth of the sample - received no training at all. Such was the use that was made of the enthusiasm of these young workers in their new employment.

Of those who received training, 74% were shown how to do their work on the job, while the remainder were trained elsewhere (most of the latter were coal miners who were trained in one of the two NCB training centres in the areas). The task of instructing the young workers in their jobs appeared to fall usually upon a fellow worker (32.6% of cases) or a supervisor (22.3% of cases). Only 18.1% of the respondents were shown how to do their jobs by a training instructor, and this was understandably only in larger organizations (e.g. The National Coal Board). 55% had completed their training when contacted 9 months into their working lives.

Given the previous willingness of respondents to undertake training for jobs, we thought it useful to examine their attitudes to training received, and to attending day or evening classes after they had begun their working lives. They were asked whether the training was useful, and all who responded to this question indicated that the training was at least of some use, with the majority(61%) classifying their training as 'very useful'. Just under one in three thought the training could have been improved. Attitudes to day and evening classes were measured using a standard attitude measurement technique. During the interview, nine months into working life, each of the young workers was handed a card on which was printed a set of 19 phrases, for example: 'No evening classes in my neighbourhood'; 'Think that more learning would be boring'; 'Would go if the firm sent me one day a week'; 'Would like to know more than I do', and they were asked to choose from the items, those which most closely represented their views about attending day or evening classes (Table 3). From the responses to this set of phrases it seemed likely that the majority would be willing to attend classes if they were relevant to the work. There were also negative responses to the idea of attending classes, nearly a quarter choosing the item 'Too tired after work', and 17% choosing the items 'had enough of school' and 'school put me off wanting any more education'. Again, 'A' band pupils in Woodbank were more positive than 'B' band pupils ('A' band - 34%; 'B' band 32.3%) and less negative ('A' band - 5.9%; 'B' band- 11.5%).

The overall attitude can perhaps best be

judged by the finding that there was an average 33.7% response to items that expressed favourable attitudes to classes (Items 3, 11, 13, 15, 16), and an average 11.6% response to the remainder of the items. This suggests that the willingness of school-leavers to train, which was expressed at school, was not just a theoretical commitment, since, having started work, the willingness to attend classes was maintained. It hints at the possibilities open to employers of utilising this obviously untapped reserve of energy, which the young workers were prepared to channel into their working lives.

3. Sex Differences In Training Received

Perhaps more disturbing, was the evidence we discovered of widespread discrimination against female school-leavers. Girls were far less likely to receive training than boys- a highly significant finding. Of the boys, 60% were given apprenticeships or formal training compared with the astonishing figure of only 14.5% amongst the girls (Table2). Girls were more likely to receive only informal training with no set length or course of instruction. These findings are highlighted by the fact that the girls in our sample were more positive in their attitudes to day and evening classes (Females - 35.5%; Males - 28.7%) and less negative (Females - 11.1%; Males - 12.3%) than were the boys. It appeared therefore that the willingness and enthusiasm of boys was being much more effectively harnessed, than was the greater enthusiasm of the girls.

The vast differences between training given to boys and girls partially reflects the deeply-rooted nature of sex discrimination in education and training, as well as in the labour market generally. Our findings are by no means idiosyncratic - as Pettman (1979) has pointed out, the imbalance in the number of girls receiving day release training from their employers, compared with boys, is as great as it has ever been. Furthermore, whilst female representation on the Government's Training Opportunities Schemes has increased considerably over the last six years, women have tended to follow only traditionally female courses, such as typing and office skills.

It might be however, that the discrepancies between training provided for boys and girls is merely due to the skills demanded by the jobs chosen by women. Over the nation as a whole, women tend to be employed largely in jobs such as catering, cleaning and hairdressing, clerical jobs, and jobs in

TABLE 3 Attitudes of young workers to the idea of attending day or evening classes

CATEGORY	% OF RESPONDENTS
1. Waste of time	4.3
2. Prefer to play sport	6.5
3. Depends on whether the classes were useful to my job	58.7
4. Too tired after work	23.9
5. Alright for the brainy ones	7.6
6. Too many things to do in my spare time	14.1
7. Don't know of any classes that would interest me	8.7
8. No evening classes in my neighbourhood	7.6
9. Find I learn a lot from talking to people at work	23.9
10. Ought to be taught all you need while you are at work	15.2
11. Would like to know more than I do	30.4
12. Think that more learning would be boring	8.7
13. Would go if the firm sent me one day a week	41.3
14. School put me off wanting any more education	17.4
15. Would go if my friends went too	8.7
16. Haven't been able to find the right kind of classes for me	5.4
17. Like to go for some things	29.3
18. Prefer to read books if I want to know anything	1.1
19. Had enough of school	17.4
N =	92

Percentages represent the percentage of respondents choosing each category

textile, clothing and footwear industries (Equal Opportunities Commission, 1978). In our survey, this general pattern was duplicated, most of the girls being employed as machinists, shopworkers or office workers (Chapter 5). It might be argued that such jobs require little formal training and that it is this fact that is responsible for the discrepancy between training for boys and training for girls.

A more likely explanation however, may be that proposed by Mednick et al, (1975). They point out that labour force participation of women tends to be intermittent and that jobs requiring training entail a perceived risk for the employer. Employers would therefore see jobs requiring little training as better alternatives for women (though such a policy ignores the fact that there is no single employment pattern for women). It would seem more likely that it is this reason, coupled with the traditional sex biases of industries and occupations, which is responsible for the large differences in training afforded the boys and girls in the present study.

4. Induction - Organizational Socialization

The induction procedures used by organizations to introduce the school-leavers to their work environment were examined by asking the young workers how much time was spent introducing them to the work and to the firm before they started actually learning their jobs. The responses to this question are shown in Table 4. Whilst one third of the sample had more than a day of introductions to the firm and the work, an identical number had no introduction at all. The remainder had introductions which varied in time from less than 30 minutes to a whole day. There were highly significant differences between sexes in the length of time spent introducing them to work and firms. Whilst nearly one half of the boys had introductions lasting over a day, less than one quarter of the girls were introduced to firms and work over a similar period of time. As a consequence, girls were more likely to start their working lives in relative ignorance of the context of their jobs. There would appear to be no rational justification for such differences. One possibility is that the discrimination (conscious or not) practised against women in industry is so pervasive that it extends even to first day induction procedures used by firms.

Overall, the large proportion of the young people who received no introduction whatsoever is a cause for disquiet. There has been much discussion in recent years of the social and psychological adjustment of people to their work settings, but, as we stressed earlier in this chapter, for young people starting work for the first time, the social and psychological adjustment required must be that much greater. Such arguments should weigh in favour of the provision of planned and formal induction courses.

TABLE 4   Time spent introducing young workers to the work and the firm

TIME	% OF RESPONDENTS	% OF MALES	% OF FEMALES
None at all	33.7	32.5	34.6
Less than 30 minutes	10.9	7.5	13.5
30 minutes to 1 hour	3.3	5.0	1.9
1 to 3 hours	3.3	0.0	5.8
Half a day	10.9	7.5	13.5
A whole day	4.3	0.0	7.7
More than a day	33.7	47.5	23.1
N =	92	40	52

5. Expectations and Realisations

Attempts were also made to discover which aspects of the job were different from the respondents' prior expectations of work. There appeared to be an even balance between favourably and unfavourably viewed aspects. Comments about unexpected aspects which were greeted favourably included:

> 'The work wasn't as hard as I expected'; 'work was more open and varied'; 'more responsibility than I expected'; 'using instruments I hadn't used before'; 'drink coffee, smoke and wander about'; 'people more friendly, work easier'; 'more easy going'; 'more interesting and able to travel'; 'better working conditions, less strict than school'.

The most frequently mentioned aspects of work, which were unexpected but welcomed, were the varied nature of the work and the easy-going atmosphere of working life. The latter aspect appeared to be compared favourably with the atmosphere of school life.

Comments about unexpected aspects of work which the respondents appeared to view unfavourably included:

> 'Travelling there takes so long'; 'the darkness and not knowing the time (coal miner)'; 'it's rotten, I'm just a fetch and carry boy, there's no respect for me'; 'harder'; 'more tiring'; 'more boring'; 'involves getting up much earlier'; 'I get put upon'; 'unfriendly, dirty and bad atmosphere'; 'harder work and the money is less'; 'very boring'.

By far the most frequent comment in this category was that the work was much harder than was originally expected, but many also commented on how boring they found the work.

Following on from this question, the young workers were asked what things they wished they had known before they started the job. Most responded to this by mentioning practical aspects of the content of the job e.g.

> 'About the materials'; 'how to lift a box properly'; 'more about the job (the most frequent response)'; 'more about wages and the quantity of work'; 'what I'd actually be doing'; 'more detail on the job and how boring it is'; 'more about machines'; 'how to put tabs on a machine'.

Details of wages and holiday arrangements were also frequently mentioned.

Finally, the respondents were asked what stood out about the first days at the job, and the responses to this question were remarkably reminiscent of the descriptions given by the young people in Carter's (1962) study in Sheffield:

> 'I was worried, trying to make a good impression'; 'I was very, very nervous and tired'; 'nervous, I didn't know anybody'; 'happy to have a job, but a bit nervous'; 'nervous and worried in case I didn't get on with the other people there'; 'everyone stared'; 'I was upset

when I made a mistake on my first letter'; 'frightened and nervous and self-conscious even though everyone was friendly'; 'being new, not knowing anyone and making silly mistakes'; 'shaky and nervous'; 'everybody was helpful and they weren't bitchy - they understood how nervous I was'; 'shy and quiet and I had to ask before I did anything all the time - the people were friendly'.

As in Carter's study, many of the youngsters mentioned how friendly people were, how some 'took the mickey out of you' and how 'everyone stares and is friendly'. The process of meeting new people and 'getting to know everybody' seemed to be of over-riding importance in the first days. Overall, the impression given was that workers went out of their way to be friendly and to make the youngsters feel welcome and at ease.

In general, therefore, our examination of school-leavers' entry into work provided both encouraging and disturbing evidence. The willingness expressed by the adolescents whilst they were still at school, to undertake lengthy periods of training for their jobs, was one of the more encouraging aspects of this study. It was perhaps surprising that so many were willing to undertake continued education whilst at the same time expressing enthusiasm at the prospect of leaving school. The attitudes held by the young workers to training courses appeared to be positive. Their predominantly favourable attitudes towards the idea of attending day or evening classes suggests that the Government's TOPS courses and Youth Opportunities Programmes would be enthusiastically received, at least in the area we studied. Our finding, that girls appeared more favourably disposed to training than boys, suggests that efforts to correct the existing imbalances in industries and occupations could be usefully supported by the provision of training courses for women, in traditionally male as well as traditionally female areas.

The results also tell us something about the importance of entry into work as a significant event in the development of the adolescent towards adulthood. Discussion of entry into work as a significant stage in human development has not been extensive, despite the acknowledgement of the practical importance of this period in young people's lives. Accordingly, it is to a discussion of entry into work that we now turn.

SOCIALIZATION TO WORK: A DEVELOPMENTAL PROCESS

Socialization during adolescence has been extensively studied in psychological and sociological research literature (see Coleman, 1979, for a review), and among the major dimensions of development identified are physical growth and maturation, intellectual development, autonomy, moral development and vocational development itself. Whilst it has been tacitly recognised that starting work in the first full-time job represents an important milestone in development, probably signifying the end of pre-adult dependency, little research has been conducted into the processes of the socialization into work of adolescents.

From a lifespan developmental perspective, beginning work in the first full-time job represents the acquisition by the young person of one of the major characteristics of adult status - the role of a worker. At an intuitive level, it seems as though this, as much as the passing of any chronological point, marks the real transition from adolescent to adult. Obviously, such a transition does not take place in a day, and it has been one of the aims of the present study to examine the period of transition from school child to working adult from a number of time perspectives. Nevertheless, if there is one point in that period which represents the most salient developmental point, it might well be the day the young person begins working life. In order to effectively operate in this new role, the young worker must learn the values, norms and required behaviours which permit him or her to participate as a member of a work organization. The learning required of the young worker is above and beyond the learning required of a worker merely changing organizations. While much research attention has been dedicated to the latter, however, very little work has been directed towards examining the socialization to working life of the adolescent.

Van Maanen (1976) has distinguished three stages in the process of socialization to work which appear to apply equally well to socialization to working life, and the use of this three stage model would be a useful starting point for such studies:

1. Anticipatory Socialization

This is defined as the degree to which an individual is prepared prior to entry into an organization (or working life) to occupy organizational positions (or working roles). Preparatory learning is seen as taking place via the person's family, peers, education and institutions and cultural influences (television, books, press etc.). Research on the transition from school to work has suggested that the majority of school-leavers are ill-prepared for working life (Jahoda, 1952; Wilson, 1953; Carter, 1962; Jahoda and Chalmers, 1963; Roberts, 1968,1970; Maizels, 1970; Hayes, 1973; Hill and Scharff, 1976; Moor, 1976; Mack, 1977) and the subjective reports of those in our survey, and their responses of surprise and bewilderment to many aspects of work add weight to these findings.

2. Entry
The second stage of the socialization to work process involves the encounter with the work environment. Hughes (1958) and Gray (1975) have proposed that when an individual enters an organization as a newly recruited member, he or she is likely to experience what Hughes calls a 'reality shock'. Those who have discussed the entry shock of recruits to organizations have emphasised that the strength of the shock will be dependent upon the accuracy with which the individual has anticipated the various expectations of the organizations. Vroom and Deci (1971) have pointed out that most learning prior to organizational entry serves to amplify and reinforce unrealistic expectations. Recruitment procedures are often devised so that information about negative features of an organization is minimised and positive features are emphasised.

3. Metamorphosis
This final stage describes the extent of personal change necessary for continuance in an organization (or in working life). During the encounter period of organizational entry, the individual begins to learn the requirements of the new role. The socializing forces of the organization will begin to reinforce those aspects of the individual's behaviour which are congruent with the aims of the organization and to punish those which are not. Thus, Schein (1964) has suggested that a process of 'unfreezing' is required because individuals enter the organization with values that are at odds with those of the organization. Forces, both formal and informal, within the organization will influence the individual towards consistency with the organization.

'The cornerstone in the theory is that a person

holding conflicting attitudes is in an uncomfortable mental state and is motivated to reduce the tension by altering his attitudes. Thus, the person is viewed as striving to adjust his attitudes so that they will be in maximum harmony'. (Van Maanen 1976)

It is this striving to adjust that is characterised as a metamorphosis.

How does this metamorphosis occur? We would argue that developmental psychology offers two theoretical approaches which aid our understanding of socialization to work. Firstly, social learning theory proposes that individuals are socialised by differential reinforcement for appropriate response. Thus, when the young worker acts in a socially approved fashion such as, for example, expressing attitudes towards management which are similar to those of the working group which he or she is a part of, then social approval follows. Similarly, other workers provide role models and exhibit behaviours which the young worker will actively attempt to learn and incorporate into his or her behavioural repertoire. Through repeated exposure, and coupled with the undeniable motivation of the young workers to be socially accepted, the process of socialization to work probably occurs at a rapid pace.

The second theoretical explanation for socialization to work is offered by cognitive developmental psychology. From this theoretical position one would view the young worker as identifying himself or herself as a coal-miner, a secretary, a nurse, a shop assistant or whatever, and then seeking to incorporate behaviours, attitudes and values appropriate to that identity. So, for example, the coal-miner may see himself as a rugged and friendly individual, since these attributes are generally valued in the mining environment. Consequently, the young worker may attempt to incorporate such attributes into his identity in order to more effectively take on the role of coalminer.

Such explanations are primarily concerned with the process of socialization to work and the advantage of combining them with Van Maanen's theory is that we have a model identifying two major processes and three stages in the process of socialization to work (see Figure 1).

It is clear that studies in this area are in need of theory to guide future research since the pattern in the past (and indeed in our study) has been to pepper young people with as many questions as was logistically possible but with little regard for theory building.

The implications of applying the theoretical constructs from organizational socialization to socialization to working life are important for those concerned with the transition from school to work period. Our research results and those of other studies suggest that young people do experience the first days at work as traumatic and disorientating. If entry to working life is to be made smoother, then thought should be given to the possibility of making that entry more gradual by the provision of realistic work experience programmes. Equally important however is that young people be given a more accurate and detailed picture of the realities of working life and the contents of jobs. Careers lessons, informal chats and the distorted images of working life presented by the media (see for example, De Fleur, 1964), are apparently inadequate, at present, in preparing young people for the new world of work.

Figure 1

Socialization to Working Life: Three Stage Process
(After Van Maanen, 1976)
---

1. Anticipatory Socialization:
   Family, peers, education,
   cultural influences.

2. Entry:
   Encounter and 'reality shock'.

3. Metamorphosis:
   Personal change necessary for continuance in working life, striving to adjust. Role models, reinforcement, cognitive developmental changes, motivation to be congruent in work environment.

SUMMARY

In an examination of attitudes to training, and training received, school-leavers were generally favourably disposed towards undertaking training, though 'B' band children from Brookvale were less willing to train for long periods. After leaving school and entering employment, girls were more likely than boys to receive only informal training or no training at all. Similarly, less time was spent introducing girls to firms and work, than was spent introducing boys. One third of the entire sample had no introduction to their firms and the work.

The young workers in our survey appeared surprised by many aspects of working life and it was clear, from their subjective reports, that the majority were apprehensive and nervous during their first days at work. These results cannot be clearly integrated with or separated from, existing theories of adolescence, and this is partially because of the paucity of both applied and theoretical work on the socialization to work of adolescents. However, one solution is to make use of theoretical constructs which have arisen from studies of organizational socialization. At the applied level, there is a need for realistic work experience programmes and realistic job previews for school-leavers.

Chapter Seven

ATTITUDES TO WORK

During the course of the research, it became apparent that two major patterns were emerging. The first was a pattern of differences in the experiences of males and females during the period, and the second was a consistent difference in the responses of adolescents from Brookvale and Woodbank.
 It became clear also, that females held different attitudes towards teachers and schools, and had dissimilar experiences from males when they entered work for the first time. It was therefore important to consider whether girls also differed from boys in their attitudes to work, and work organizations, once they had left school. This was not merely an academic question, since the possibility that the attitudes and experiences of males and females differ throughout the transition period, has far-reaching implications for education, careers teaching and selection.
 A consistent picture of differences in the reports of Woodbank and Brookvale pupils was also being formed as questionnaire responses were analysed. In searching for causes for these different responses, one factor had emerged as important, that of school organization and ethos. Woodbank was organised into academic streams which were grouped in the 'A' band (for brighter pupils) and the 'B' band. The ethos of the school also seemed to reflect the conflict which the banding system appeared to generate, with greater hostility expressed towards teachers, and greater rivalry between groups of pupils being more characteristic of Woodbank school. However, the influence of the schools appeared to extend beyond the school walls. Differences in attitudes to training for jobs had emerged, which appeared to be linked to the banding

system employed in Woodbank. It is not a far cry from this to speculate that experiences in school life might have effects also upon attitudes to work. For example, it might be that attitudes towards the school as an organization could be the prototype for attitudes towards work organizations. Thus, pupils resentful of their schools as organizations, might carry these resentments over into their working life. This, in turn, might have a potent effect upon their happiness and satisfaction in full-time employment.

Differences between the schools also suggested that pupils from Woodbank school had much higher expectations of the world of work. We were therefore interested to discover whether the frustrations they experienced on beginning work, had significant and lasting effects upon their attitudes to working life. Again, these are not merely academic questions. If adolescents who leave school with unrealistic expectations of working life feel dissatisfied or resentful in their jobs, then there is a real need to discover how expectations are raised in this way.

Apart from group differences in attitudes of school-leavers to work, it is important also to investigate such things as how attitudes to work change over time. For example, do adolescents' attitudes to work crystallise shortly after they begin work and then remain relatively static? Or, alternatively, do they change and, if so, do attitudes become more positive or more negative? How do young people perceive their work? What do they like most and what do they like least? How ambitious are they and how settled do they feel in their jobs, having started work? Is feeling settled related to achieving occupational aims or does it have more to do with having a happy social life at work? These are all questions to which psychologists, careers officers, teachers and employers need answers, if the transition of school-leavers to working life is to be understood. It is worth emphasising that, for most school-leavers, entry into work represents their first experience of full-time employment. It also represents their first experience of the kind of activity which is likely to occupy a large proportion of the rest of their lives. Their reactions to this experience and their attitudes to work can tell us a good deal about their perceptions of their present quality of life, as well as about how they see their futures.

Previous studies of the transition from school to work have generally been of two kinds. One involves the use of retrospective questionnaire surveys, in which people are invited to report on their experiences of the transition from school to work, after the transition is over. This method suffers from the disadvantage that people often forget important bits of information and tend to see their past experiences in terms of the way in which they see the world at present. In other words, such procedures are often contaminated by quirks of memory. The second kind of study - longitudinal research - involves repeated measurements of experiences during the transition period, and so does not incorporate the disadvantages associated with retrospective assessment. However, previous longitudinal studies of transition from school to work, have only investigated experiences of school-leavers on one occasion before leaving school, and on one occasion after leaving school. The results provided by these longitudinal studies have been extremely valuable, but they have told us nothing about whether school-leavers attitudes to work change with their experience of work. A major aim of the present survey therefore, was to examine attitudes to work more than once, and to discover whether they changed over time. Along with this aim we were also concerned to examine group differences - differences between males and females, and between Woodbank and Brookvale students.

RESULTS

1. Attitudes to Work Over Time

At 9 months into their working lives, the young workers were asked to describe how they felt about their jobs i.e. whether they liked them, were indifferent to them, hated them etc. Most indicated that they liked their jobs (Table 1), though more than one in six were either indifferent to their jobs or actively disliked the work they were doing. At 30 months into their working lives, this question was repeated. There proved to be a significant relationship between attitudes to work, and time into working life (Table 1). The young workers reported liking their jobs more, and disliking their jobs less, the longer they progressed into working life. At nine months after leaving school, 36.8% of those who replied to the question said that they loved their jobs, but by 30 months 47.1% of the sample responded in this way.

These results could be explained by arguing that the adolescents began their working lives with mistaken, and possibly inflated expectations of the quality and content of working life. If this was so, one would expect young people to be less happy with their jobs early in working life, since they would be going through a period of adjustment or disillusionment. However, a closer examination of the results led us to a somewhat different conclusion. At nine months into working life, the females were significantly less likely than the males in the sample, to express strong positive attitudes towards work, and significantly, more likely to express strong negative attitudes (Table 1). Thus, at nine months, nearly half of the males said that they liked their work, compared with about one in four of the females. Moreover, whereas none of the boys reported hating their jobs at this time, 13.5% of the girls did so.

These results suggested therefore, that for girls, the early experience of work was far less favourable than the early experience of boys. We would see as the most likely explanation of these sex differences, the greater discrepancy between the expectations of the world of work, and the reality experienced by the females, in comparison with the males in our survey. It may well be that the quality of working life of women entering the world of work, is poorer than that of males. Certainly, the prevalence of discrimination against women in the world of work is well established (see for example Hunt, 1975), and this discrimination is likely to be experienced by young women immediately they begin their working lives. Training and induction procedures for women in industry are more likely to be informal or non-existent than they are for men (Chapter 6). The lack of training communicates to women something about the value of their work to their employers, and does nothing to enhance job-satisfaction or self-esteem in young women beginning their working lives. A combination of these factors can therefore have detrimental effects upon women's attitudes to work, at the start of their working lives.

When the attitudes to work of males and females were measured at 30 months into working life, it was discovered that the sex differences evident at nine months, had disappeared. At 30 months into working life 50% of the women reported loving their work (compared with 26.9% at nine months). This highly significant change in the females' attitudes to work appeared to be accounted for largely by respondents who had previously reported only liking

TABLE 1 School-leavers' attitudes to work at nine months and thirty months into their working lives

CATEGORY	% ALL SCHOOL-LEAVERS 9 MONTHS	% ALL SCHOOL-LEAVERS 30 MONTHS	% MALES 9 MONTHS	% MALES 30 MONTHS	% FEMALES 9 MONTHS	% FEMALES 30 MONTHS
I love it	36.8	47.1	48.0	43.9	26.9	50.0
I am enthusiastic about it / I like it	45.3	27.6	39.0	26.8	50.0	28.3
I am indifferent to it	6.3	16.1	11.0	22.0	3.8	10.9
I don't like it	4.2	6.9	2.0	4.9	5.8	8.7
I dislike it / I hate it	7.4	2.3	0.0	2.4	13.5	2.2
Total =	95	87	43	41	52	46

their jobs,becoming more enthusiastic. The number who were indifferent to, or disliked their jobs, remained nearly the same.

The males in the sample however, appeared to show a change in attitudes to work, over time, in the opposite direction, though this change was not nearly as large as that shown by the female workers. At nine months into working life only 13% of males were indifferent to, or actually disliked their work. By 30 months this figure had risen to nearly 30% of the males in the survey. At nine months, 11% of males reported that they were indifferent to their work, but by 30 months into working life, this figure had doubled to 22%. Similarly, whereas only 3.8% of females had been indifferent to their jobs at nine months, 16.1% were indifferent to their work at 30 months into their working lives (Table 1).

What seemed to be happening was that, as the young people experienced more of working life, a minority (mostly females) became more enthusiastic, but a large number of both males and females became more indifferent to their work, neither liking nor disliking it.At the same time there is less of a discrepancy between male and female attitudes to work, the further into working life they are assessed. The lack of a sex difference at 30 months is explicable in terms of the adjustment of attitudes which occur during socialization to work (Chapter 6).Thus, we would see the young female worker as holding conflicting attitudes - expecting more of working life than she perceives herself receiving, yet at the same time expecting to be moderately satisfied in working life. The possible resolution of such a conflict would then lie either in changing jobs, or in altering attitudes. We have proposed (Chapter 10) that job changing does occur and that, as a result, more realistic expectations of working life are fostered, since available alternative jobs are found,on average, to be no more satisfying.It is also likely that the tension created by the conflict is reduced by the individual altering her attitudes and expectations.Attitudes and expectations would then be expected to change in the direction either of greater liking e.g.'Now I know the job better I really love the work' or in the direction of indifference - e.g. 'I used to hate the job at first, but now I just while away the time by chatting'.In the latter case, what may be happening is that those who originally hated their jobs, find other sources of gratification (e.g.social interaction) and become merely indifferent to their work. Thus, one would expect there to less of a discrepancy between male and female attitudes to work, the further into working life they are assessed.

This does not explain of course, why males should become indifferent to their work, the further into working life they progress. We would see the following explanation as most convincing: males leave school with relatively high expectations of working life, knowing, for example, that working life is likely to confer upon them the status of adult. Early in working life males are trained and given responsibility, and, more so than females, the realities of working life live up to their expectations. However, once initial skills are learned and the job mastered, work is often simply monotonous and unchallenging. Indeed, many of the respondents described their jobs as boring(see below).After the initial excitement and novelty of working life are over, the reality of days of boredom perhaps begins to set in. Males might therefore like their jobs more early in working life than females, because of the higher levels of skill, training and responsibility required, but, after this novelty has worn off, their attitudes to work might begin to drift towards indifference.

Therefore, whilst an initial examination of our results suggests that the respondents tended to like their work more as they progressed into working life, closer analysis reveals that there was an underlying trend towards greater indifference.

2. School-leavers' Descriptions of Their Jobs

A number of questions were directed at discovering the most salient characteristics of their jobs as perceived by the young workers. Information gained included details of workplaces, how closely respondents worked with others, how clear they were of what was expected of them at work, difficulty of work, amount of work, pressure of work, and intrinsic job interest. Distributions of workplaces of jobs was quite wide for the males who were represented in all categories (Table 2). Females however, were employed almost entirely in shops, offices or factories, 80% alone working in either offices or factories. This finding reflects the greater diversity of employment possibilities available to males. The majority of respondents (62.4%) worked very closely with other people in their jobs and only a small minority (5.4%) worked completely alone. Similarly, a majority was completely clear of what was expected of them at work most of the time (80%) and the remainder was clear either half the time (13%) or only occasionally (7%). There were no group differences in responses to these questions nor in perceived difficulty of jobs. Of the respondents, 57% found their jobs very easy or quite easy and only 14.9% found their jobs either somewhat difficult or quite difficult.

Questions concerning the amount of work revealed that most respondents felt that there was usually just about the right amount to do (67.9%) and that there was generally a fair amount of variety in their work (76.6%). About half of the time 44.3% reportedly worked under high pressure and 36.4% were 'pretty relaxed most of the time'. Again, there were no group differences in response to these questions.

3. Perceived Job Interest

At nine months into working life, all the subjects were asked about how interesting they found their jobs. The vast majority (85%) found their jobs at least 'somewhat interesting', 41.5% finding them 'very interesting'. However, in the replies to this question there were highly significant sex differences (Table 3). Females were less likely to describe job interest in strong positive terms. Whilst 62% of the men described their jobs as 'very interesting', only 25% of the women described their jobs in the same way (Table 3). Similarly, whilst only 7.2% of males found their jobs boring, over one in five females did so. This conforms with the previous finding of less favourable attitudes to work amongst women, and suggests that they may have expected more interesting jobs, or that work itself would be a more interesting environment than they found to be the case. It is unlikely that initial expectations differ between males and females (there is no evidence that this is so), but more likely that it is the kind of work they do which differs. Alternatively, females may be less happy in working life than males generally, because of a variety of reasons (e.g. lower job status, rates of pay, conditions etc.), and may therefore be less likely to express strong positive attitudes towards any aspect of work. To examine this question in more detail, it would be interesting to carry out objective assessments of job interest by conducting a study of jobs taken by a large sample of male and female school-leavers and deriving independent assessments of intrinsic interest. These findings also add credence to our interpretation of sex differences in attitudes to work described above.

If women's work is less interesting (or even perceived as less interesting) then it would be understandable that women entering work for the first time, would have less favourable attitudes than males towards work, at least early in their working lives.

The young workers were also asked to describe those aspects of their jobs which they liked least and those which they like most. Aspects liked appeared to fall into five major categories, of which, the most important appeared to be the 'social' category (Appendix F). This included responses such as:

> 'You meet all kinds of people'; 'I like my friends there'; 'The girls I work with'; 'there are people around to talk to'; 'It's a good friendly atmosphere'; 'working with people'; 'the small friendly office'; 'the young man I work with'.

Responses falling into this category accounted for nearly half of all the responses to the question, and this adds support to Hayes' (1973) contention that more attention should be paid to giving information in schools, on the psycho-social aspects of occupations, since it is these aspects which appear to be important in young people's positive perceptions of their jobs. Interest in features of the job itself however, was also a frequently mentioned 'most-liked' aspect of work, e.g.

> 'The electrical knowledge I'm getting'; 'the work is interesting'; 'I'm learning something different every day'; 'the actual hairdressing'; 'serving on the counter'.

In contrast, features of the jobs also accounted for 19% of aspects most disliked, with boredom and menial tasks accounting for a further 23%. Some respondents mentioned bosses and co-workers as disliked aspects but pay, working conditions and hours of work also figured prominently amongst aspects disliked. If employers are interested in increasing satisfaction amongst young workers, providing more interesting work and more opportunities for social contact during work are two obvious ways in which this can be accomplished.

4. School-leavers' Job Characteristics

In order to assess perceived job characteristics in

TABLE 2   Distribution of workplaces of jobs of respondents

CATEGORY	% OF RESPONDENTS	% OF MALES	% OF FEMALES
In an office	23.6	9.5	35.3
In a factory	34.4	21.4	45.1
In a shop	12.9	7.1	17.6
Travelling	1.1	2.4	0.0
Down the pit	6.5	14.3	0.0
Outside	7.5	16.7	0.0
Other	14.0	28.6	2.0
N =	93	42	51

TABLE 3   Job interest attributed by respondents to their jobs

CATEGORY	% OF RESPONDENTS	% OF MALES	% OF FEMALES
Very interesting	41.5	61.9	25.0
Quite "	29.8	19.0	38.5
Somewhat "	13.8	11.9	15.4
Somewhat boring	5.3	2.4	7.7
Quite boring	3.2	0.0	5.7
Very boring	6.4	4.8	7.7
N =	94	42	52

a more detailed and objective way and so that the results might be statistically analysed, the young workers were asked to select, from a check list of 31 items, those which applied to their present jobs (Appendix F: Tables 2,3,4). This checklist has previously been used by Maizels (1970) in her study of school to work transition. In addition to the items used in previous studies, we added a further three: 'competitive', 'nimble fingers' and 'too heavy'. These three items produced low response rates but appeared to distinguish quite well between characteristics of jobs perceived to be salient by males and females. Following Maizels (1970) we divided responses into four main groups: 'interest', 'demand', 'physical' and 'social' factors associated with each job.

a) Interest (see Appendix F: Table 2). Seven items were deemed to indicate characteristics likely to increase the interest of young workers in their job e.g. 'chance to use initiative', 'varied', 'uses brains', 'skilled'; and four items as likely to diminish interest e.g. 'too routine', 'monotonous', 'not enough skill'. The percentages of responses to each item reported by Maizels were examined and the correlation between the percentages in her study and in the present study was found to be high and positive. This suggests consistency in the relative salience for young workers, of the items in the checklist.

As in Maizels' study, slightly less than half of the respondents described their jobs as interesting, though considerably more in the present survey indicated that their jobs were varied (45% as against 27% in Maizels' study). Fewer than one fifth described their work as skilled or as using their brains. At the same time, the respondents were much more likely to choose positive interest items than negative interest items, when describing their jobs.

A comparison of workers from Brookvale and Woodbank revealed that workers who had previously attended Brookvale school were more likely to describe their jobs as having positive interest characteristics, than workers who had previously attended Woodbank school (a highly significant finding). It is possible that such a finding is related to the greater incidence of discrepancies between occupational aims at school and ultimate attainments, evident amongst those who attended Woodbank school. It might be, for example, that because their initial expectations were higher than their attainments, that they would view their work - at least at first - as holding less interest for them than the jobs that they had originally aimed for. This finding also conforms to the interpretation that Woodbank pupils had higher expectations of the world of work, because of the implicit assumption within Woodbank, that conscientious work at school would be rewarded by interesting work at the end of school life.

A comparison of males' and females' responses to the items showed that whilst there were no overall statistically significant differences between the sexes, the women did appear less likely to see their jobs as holding positive interest and were more likely to describe their jobs in negative interest terms. For example, if items 3 and 4 ('have to concentrate', 'interesting product/service') are ignored as being more factual descriptions than value judgements, differences between the sexes on positive interest items are significant (Appendix F: Table 2). Such a finding is consistent with the results reported above, of sex differences in perceived intrinsic job interest.

b) Demand and Physical (Appendix F: Table 3). Six items were included to indicate the physical and other demands on young workers of the jobs performed e.g. 'keeps you busy', 'pause when you want to', 'responsible';and eight items were included to indicate the physical environment of the work e.g. 'mainly indoors', 'noisy', 'clean', 'mainly sitting'. Again the percentage of responses to items reported in Maizels' study were examined and the correlation between these percentages, and those reported in the present study, was positive and significant.

A majority of the young workers described their jobs as keeping them busy, but at the same time only 15% characterised their work as difficult. Of the respondents, 40% perceived their jobs as 'responsible'. There were no significant differences between schools or sexes overall, though on individual items clear sex differences did emerge. For example, males were more likely than females to see their jobs as competitive, and less likely to describe their jobs as needing nimble fingers. Females were much more likely to have jobs that involved mainly sitting, and less likely to have jobs that were 'dirty'.

Respondents from the 'A' band of Woodbank school characterised their jobs as more demanding and more physical than did respondents from the 'B' band. This appeared to be a difference between groups in number of items chosen overall however, since those respondents who were originally 'A' band pupils tended to choose more items describing work overall, than did those who were originally 'B' band pupils. On average, for each item, 30.8% of 'A' band responded, compared with only 22.1% of 'B' band.

c) Social and status characteristics (Appendix F: Table 4). Five items were included in this category which described the social and status characteristics of the jobs e.g. 'Work with a good crowd', 'offers promotion prospects', 'well paid'. As in Maizels' study, there was a much higher response rate to these items, than to items in the 'interest' or 'demand and physical' categories of job characteristics. This suggests that young people perceive and describe their jobs more in terms of such social and status characteristics. It may well be that they will also evaluate their jobs in terms of these characteristics.

The item 'work with a good crowd' produced the largest percentage of responses of all the items on the checklist, though only one quarter of the respondents indicated that they worked with people of their own age group. All the items in this category (excepting perhaps, 'work with own age group') are positively value laden, e.g. work with a _good_ crowd; teaching me something _useful_; _well_ paid. The high overall response rate to these items confirms that the young workers tended to characterise their jobs more in positive than in negative terms.

Respondents who had previously attended Woodbank school described their jobs in significantly less 'social' terms than those who had previously attended Brookvale school. They were much less likely to see their jobs as teaching them something useful (Woodbank - 25%; Brookvale - 47.1%) and as offering promotion prospects (Woodbank - 21.2%; Brookvale - 47.1%). Taken together with the finding described above, that Woodbank students were less likely than Brookvale students to describe their jobs as having positive interest characteristics, this suggests that Woodbank students were less satisfied generally with their jobs than were Brookvale students. This greater dissatisfaction, as measured by responses to the social and status items of the checklist, may be related to the fact that Woodbank students took jobs of significantly

lower status than they had hoped for (see Chapter 5).
We have already discussed the possible antecedents
for this difference between schools in status of
jobs aimed at, and attained, both in terms of
school organization (i.e. a banded system vs an
unbanded system) and in terms of careers teaching
(developmental vs differential approaches). If
these factors are responsible for the differences
between pupils from the two schools in attitudes to
their work, the implications for school organization
and/or careers teaching are considerable.

Female workers were less likely than males to
see their jobs as offering promotion prospects.
Generally however, the females in our survey were
unlikely to have jobs offering good promotion
prospects. Maizels (1970) also found that females
were significantly less likely than males to have
good promotion chances, as rated by both employers
and school-leavers themselves. The female workers in
the present study tended not to see their jobs as
teaching them something useful. The relative
scarcity of formal training for female school-
leavers may have led the women to the conclusion
that their work was not teaching them anything useful, since it did not require training.

Former 'A' band pupils were also more likely to
see their jobs as offering promotion prospects
(38.9%) than former 'B' band pupils (14.3%). Again,
lack of promotion prospects for 'B' band pupils may
have been as much a matter of fact as an expression
of attitudes to work.

5. Hours and Pay

Along a number of dimensions relating to conditions
of employment, females' experience of work-life
differed drastically from that of males. Whereas
40% of males reported working overtime most weeks,
only 27% of females did so. Females were also less
likely to work weekends and less likely than males
to have any additional benefits from their work,
such as extra money, or benefits like travel
expenses and luncheon vouchers. Whereas 47% of the
males had such benefits, only 27% of the females
reported receiving them. Such subtle forms of
discrimination must contribute in no small way
towards the greater dissatisfaction and unhappiness
of women in working life. More important, perhaps,
the way wages were worked out also differed significantly between the sexes. Nearly one third of the
females in the sample were paid on a piecework
system. Very often females working in the textile

industry were paid according to the amount of work they produced. However, if there was no work immediately available their pay was considerably reduced. None of the males was paid in this way (Table 4).

There proved to be a significant relationship between the sex of a worker and pay. Females were less likely to be highly paid and more likely to be low paid than males (Table 5). Fewer than 10% of males were paid less than 21 pounds per week whereas more than one in four females were paid below this figure. At the top end of the scale 16% of males were paid more than 39 pounds per week. None of the females was paid this amount. This evidence of discrimination further reinforces the view that the world of work entered by females is very different and much less desirable, than the world of work of the male.

6. Job Stability and Ambitions

At nine months into their working lives, the young workers were asked how interested they were in being promoted or in changing jobs at their present places of work, and 65.8% indicated a positive interest. Their replies also showed that nearly 85% felt that their chances of promotion in their present jobs were quite good or very good. Nearly a third of respondents were considering changing their jobs within the year but only 11% indicated that they felt unsettled in their present jobs.

Respondents who had formerly attended Woodbank school were far more likely to be considering a change of job (46%) than former Brookvale students (14%) and the relationship between this factor and schools was statistically significant (Table 6). Similarly, there was a significant relationship between schools and responses to the question 'how settled do you feel in your present job?'. Again, Woodbank students appeared to be less settled in their jobs than students from Brookvale school. These findings provide further strong evidence of the greater dissatisfaction with their jobs amongst former Woodbank students. There were no differences between the bands within Woodbank in response to these questions.

The women in our survey were significantly less likely to be interested in promotion or in changing jobs at their places of work than were the males (Table 7). This difference probably reflects again the lack of real possibilities of promotion for many of the women in the sample. At the same time, the women appeared to feel less settled in their jobs than males, only 34% indicating that they felt very settled, compared with 56% of males.

SUMMARY AND CONCLUSIONS

In this examination of young workers' attitudes to work, the two trends referred to at the beginning of the chapter were again consistently evident. The first was for females to have markedly different attitudes and experiences from those of males during the transition from school to work. Females were less happy early in their working lives than males; they were less likely to describe their feelings about their jobs in strongly favourable ways than were males; they found their jobs less interesting than did males; they were lower paid; they were more likely to be paid on a piecework system and were less likely to have the chance of, or to be considering promotion. It is therefore evident that the females experienced far greater disillusionment on beginning their working lives than males. Perhaps the simplest explanation for these sex differences is that the lot of the women at work in the present survey, was worse than that of the men. Lower pay and payment on a piecework system are objectively worse than higher payment and fixed rate payments, particularly where the quantity of available work is variable. Discrimination was not restricted to pay however. On a national scale, there is evidence that discrimination against women is pervasive in industry. For example, Hunt (1975) found that a majority of those responsible for hiring employees, in her survey of management attitudes and practices towards women, start off with the belief that a woman applicant is likely to be inferior to a man in respect of all qualities considered to be important. We would see such discrimination as related to the sex differences in attitudes to work in this survey. The failure to provide channels of promotion for women must leave many feeling frustrated or helpless, of which both reactions serve to reduce the quality of working life. The generally poorer quality of life for women at work inevitably leads them to have less favourable attitudes. The only alternative, and rather less plausible explanation, is that the females in our study left school with higher expectations of working life than did the males.

The second trend was for pupils who had attended Woodbank school to have different attitudes

TABLE 4 Type of wage paid to young workers

CATEGORY	% RESPONDENTS	% MALE	% FEMALE
Piecework	17.4	0.0	31.3
Hourly	15.2	26.8	5.9
Fixed	60.9	65.9	56.9
Other	6.5	7.3	5.9
N =	92	41	51

TABLE 5 Weekly wage of young workers

WAGES IN POUNDS	% RESPONDENTS	% MALE	% FEMALE
13 - 20	18.3	9.1	26.5
21 - 30	57.0	56.8	57.2
31 - 39	17.2	18.2	16.3
39 +	7.5	15.9	0.0
N =	93	44	49

TABLE 6 Percentages of school-leavers considering changing their jobs, and percentages feeling settled in their jobs

CATEGORY	% RESPONDENTS	% WOODBANK	% BROOKVALE
Changing jobs			
Definitely	19.8	30.2	9.3
Perhaps	10.5	16.3	4.7
No	69.7	53.5	86.0
N =	86	43	43
Settled in jobs			
Very settled	44.0	33.3	54.3
Quite settled	30.7	26.7	34.8
Fairly settled	14.3	22.2	6.5
Not very settled	4.4	8.9	0.0
Not at all settled	6.6	8.9	4.4
N =	91	45	46

TABLE 7 Percentages of school-leavers interested in promotion or in changing jobs at their places of work

INTEREST IN PROMOTION OR CHANGING JOBS	% RESPONDENTS	% MALES	% FEMALES
Yes	65.8	81.6	51.2
No	34.2	18.4	48.8
Total =	79	38	41

from those of former Brookvale pupils. Former pupils of Woodbank school found their jobs less interesting than did workers who had attended Brookvale; they saw their jobs as offering them less in the way of promotion prospects, pay, useful learning or even social contacts; they were also less settled in their jobs and more likely to be considering changing their jobs.

This coherent picture of greater dissatisfaction amongst former Woodbank pupils is not easily explicable in terms of a single causal factor. One important difference between the two schools however, was that the careers teaching followed very differing lines (see Chapter 1), and it might be argued that the style of careers teaching in Woodbank where it was suggested that work chosen should be consistent with one's 'self-concept' as a worker, produced heightened expectations of the world of work, which were not congruent with the reality. If this was so, then it would be expected that the experience of the world of work would be less satisfying for Woodbank children than for Brookvale children.

Another major difference between the two schools was the emphasis on academic values and the stress laid upon the rewards of hard work. Thus, the covert propoganda within the school may have given credence to the idea that by working hard at school, one's lot in working life would be better. The effects of this might then have been to raise expectations of working life throughout the school, with even 'B' band students being affected by the optimism of the 'A' band. Our finding that the Woodbank pupils had to take jobs of significantly lower status than they had originally aimed at, suggests that by some means, expectations of working life were raised more amongst Woodbank pupils than they were amongst pupils of Brookvale school.

The interpretations proposed here are, of course, speculative, and the discovery of the causative factor or factors will depend upon the outcome of controlled research, which might isolate the significant features of school life which affect later attitudes to work.

The transition from school to work represents the first full-time experience of a way of life which will occupy a large proportion of the rest of the adolescent's life. Our findings suggest that the first experience of some groups of school-leavers is not happy, and that the further into working life they progress, the more indifferent to their jobs many young workers learn to become.

Chapter Eight

ATTITUDES TO SUPERVISORS

The importance of attitudes of young workers to their supervisors is in many ways self evident but, in addition, the extent to which the individual has settled into the world of work may be related partially to his or her perceived relationships with supervisors. As Rutter et al (1979) have pointed out, there is a relationship between people's work and behaviour in institutional settings, and their attitudes to those in charge. Thus, Kahn and Katz (1960) found that employees who saw their supervisors as understanding of their difficulties, concerned about their problems and needs, and interested in them as individuals, were more highly productive. The study of young workers' attitudes to supervisors therefore, is important not just for its intrinsic interest, but also in the light it casts on our understanding of the process of transition to work, on the socialization to work of young people, and on the relationship between school experience and early work experience and attitudes.

In any discussion of the relationship between employers and employees, or between work supervisors and workers, there is a danger of making value assumptions which can bias both the interpretation of results, and the understanding of the phenomenon under investigation. For example, if we say it is important for young people to begin working life with favourable attitudes towards supervisors, we are open to attack from those who may wish to motivate workers to resist repressive work practices of employers. Alternatively, if we argue that workers should be aware of the repression of the work force by profit-maximising capitalists, we are open to the criticism that we are allowing political values to affect our scientific analysis. It is impossible to exclude political and moral biases from social survey research altogether, but it is possible and necessary to be aware of their existence. In any study of the transition from school to work, an awareness of these dangers is vital.

The attitudes to supervisors of the young workers in the present study were measured by using a checklist adopted by Maizels (1970), from a National Institute of Industrial Psychology study of job satisfaction (Handyside, 1961). This checklist was also used to measure the attitudes of the young people to their teachers, while they were still at school. In this case, using a longitudinal research design, afforded us the valuable opportunity of comparing attitudes to teachers and attitudes to supervisors as measured by the same scale.

Before the checklist was given to the respondents however, two global questions were asked, in order to provide a comparative measure of attitudes to supervisors. Firstly, the young workers were asked: 'Thinking about your mates/colleagues at work, would you say they are very easy, quite easy, somewhat difficult or very difficult to get on with?'. The majority (91%) indicated that their co-workers were very or quite easy to get on with. However, former Brookvale students appeared to judge their co-workers in significantly more positive terms than did workers who had previously attended Woodbank (the banded school), only 42% of the latter describing co-workers as very easy to get on with, compared with 67% from Brookvale (Table 1). The same question was then asked in relation to supervisors,and there were no differences between the responses to the two questions - 55.3% describing co-workers as very easy to get on with and 48.9% describing supervisors as very easy to get on with. Again however,there was a difference between responses of former Brookvale and former Woodbank students. Those from Brookvale were significantly more positive in their descriptions of relations with supervisors - 60% describing them as very easy to get on with, compared with only 36.4% from Woodbank (see Table 1).

The attitude cheklist was then administered by presenting the young workers with a card on which a number of descriptive items were listed in random order (e.g. 'explains things clearly', 'considerate', 'helpful', 'muddled'). The respondents were asked to choose the items which described the person (or people) most in charge of their work. They were told that they could choose as many items as they

TABLE 1 Young workers' descriptions of their relations with co-workers and supervisors

CATEGORY	CO-WORKERS			SUPERVISORS		
	TOTAL %	WOODBANK %	BROOKVALE %	TOTAL %	WOODBANK %	BROOKVALE %
Very easy to get on with	55.3	42.2	67.3	48.9	36.4	60.4
Quite easy to get on with	36.2	48.9	24.5	38.0	50.0	27.1
Somewhat difficult to get on with	6.4	6.7	6.1	8.7	9.1	8.3
Very difficult to get on with	2.1	2.2	2.0	4.3	4.5	4.2
N =	94	45	49	92	44	48

wished. The percentages of respondents choosing each item are shown in Appendix G. As in Chapter 2, the items were divided into positive and negative evaluations of supervisors, and into evaluations of their professional and personal qualities (after Maizels, 1970). Overall, the young workers were likely to describe supervisors more in positive terms than in negative terms. Over 60% described their supervisor as knowing his or her job and 52% said their supervisors were good to work under. The most frequently chosen negative item - 'moody' - was chosen by 20% of respondents. Whereas, on average, each positive item was chosen by 34% of the young workers, an average of only 9% chose each negative item.

When comparisons were made between the percentages of items chosen to describe teachers at school and supervisors at work, a significant relationship was found. At the same time, the respondents were significantly more favourable in descriptions of supervisors than they had been in their descriptions of teachers, and significantly less unfavourable (in that they chose fewer negative items) in their descriptions of supervisors. Thus, whereas only 20% described teachers as 'good to work for', more than 50% described supervisors as 'good to work under'. Similarly, over 60% described supervisors as knowing their jobs, whereas only a third described their teachers in this way. Also, whilst 25% had described teachers as 'sarcastic', only 14% saw their supervisors as displaying this characteristic.

It is interesting to note that whereas respondents expressed positive perceptions of teachers more in personal terms, e.g. 'kind', 'sincere' etc., they tended to express positive perceptions of supervisors more in relation to their professional characteristics e.g. 'knows his or her job', 'good to work under', 'efficient' (Appendix G, Table 3).

Former students of Brookvale school were consistently more positive in evaluations of supervisors in terms of both personal and professional characteristics. This result is particularly interesting in the light of the earlier finding that pupils from Brookvale were more positive in evaluations of teachers than pupils from Woodbank school. In particular, former Brookvale students were more likely to describe their supervisors as encouraging them, clever (items relating to professional characteristics) helpful and fair (items relating to personal characteristics). There were no differences between the two groups in negative items chosen to describe supervisors. There appeared to be no other group differences in attitudes to supervisors i.e. between bands or sexes.

SUMMARY OF RESULTS

1. Of the respondents, 91% reported that their co-workers were easy or very easy to get on with; 87% of the respondents reported that their supervisors were easy or very easy to get on with.
2. Significant positive correlations were found between the results of the survey and the results of Maizels' (1970) survey on items chosen to describe characteristics of supervisors.
3. Significant positive correlations were found between attitudes to teachers and attitudes to supervisors.
4. Respondents were significantly more favourable in descriptions of supervisors than they were in descriptions of teachers, and were significantly more unfavourable in descriptions of teachers than they were in descriptions of supervisors.
5. Whereas respondents had weighted favourable descriptions of teachers more on personal characteristics, they tended to weight favourable descriptions of supervisors more on professional characteristics (e.g. knows his/her job).
6. Former Brookvale pupils were more likely to describe co-workers and supervisors as very easy to get on with, than were former Woodbank students. They were also more likely than former Woodbank students to choose items describing favourable characteristics of supervisors.

Attitudes to supervisors therefore appeared favourable, when both global questions and detailed item checklists were used to measure them. Comparisons of attitudes to co-workers, and attitudes to supervisors also revealed that supervisors were described in relatively favourable ways. Perhaps most striking however, was the finding that attitudes to supervisors were consistently more favourable and less unfavourable than attitudes to teachers had been.

How far are the attitudes expressed a true reflection of the real attitudes of the young workers? The item checklist used in Maizels' survey and in the present study does appear to be reliable. Correlations between measures produced by the checklist in different situations and at different times are positive and significant. More important however is the question of validity. To what extent is the item checklist a valid predictor or measure of attitudes to teachers and supervisors?

No examinations of the relationship between answers to this checklist and other measures of attitudes to supervisors (or teachers) have been reported in the literature. It is therefore impossible to state the accuracy of the test instrument as a measure of true attitudes to teachers and supervisors. There is certainly a need for investigating attitudes to teachers and supervisors in more depth, using more sophisticated and detailed measures than could be included in the already large battery of questions used in the present survey. But perhaps what can be drawn fairly safely from the results is that, in our sample of young people, in relation to characteristics listed on the checklist, broad differences in attitudes to teachers and supervisors did appear to exist.

It may be argued that the attitudes of the young people to their supervisors were favourable only because they had just started work. We have argued (see Chapter 9) that working life may appear to be a new and glamorous change in status from school child to working adult, and that, for many young people, there is the feeling that beginning work is the beginning of adult life and independence, which involves freedom from the rules and restrictions of school. If this is true, it is possible that supervisors are also viewed as part of this new and glamorous world and are therefore viewed in favourable ways. The hypothesis that supervisors are viewed favourably by young workers because they represent one aspect of a whole new world viewed, at least initially, as a glamorous change, is one which is more easily subject to empirical test.

Changes in attitudes to supervisors could be measured longitudinally and compared for example, with changes in attitudes to co-workers. Certainly it is important that changes in attitudes are examined anyway, in order that the process of socialization to work of young people be better understood.

It may be that supervisors are favourably viewed because of a happy contrast between relationships with supervisors and relationships with teachers. Teachers at school exercise a wider authority over pupils than do supervisors in the work situation. The former have powers of direction over more 'personal' as well as work-oriented behaviour. Pupils can be told to dress in a certain way, stay late after school, not to chew or 'smirk' or not to talk to other pupils at various points in the school day. On occasions they may be subjected to physical reprimand by caning. Such authority is far greater than the authority of supervisors who, whilst they may have many forms of social control available to them, have much less control over the 'personal' behaviours of workers. Thus, it might be argued that attitudes to supervisors and teachers differ because the relationship between supervisors and workers is characterised by a greater degree of individual freedom, where the rules are changed, and possibly, where the relationship itself is more straight-forward. The worker is expected to work for the immediate reward of pay and the sanction of dismissal is more powerful and relevant to the individual's life. The pupil on the other hand, has to work for deferred reward (examination success), and sanctions such as 'detention', 'lines', 'tellings-off' etc. may have little relevance to the pupil's life generally.

This argument would be consistent also with the finding that the young workers expressed favourable attitudes to supervisors in terms more of professional characteristics than of personal characteristics (in contrast to descriptions of teachers). This would be explained by the interpretation that teachers exercise more control over the personal behaviour of pupils, whereas the relationship between a supervisor and a young worker is restricted more to the domain of the professional i.e. behaviour to do with the work itself, rather than any personal characteristics of the worker. This de-emphasis of 'personal' behaviour, as being under the control of the authority figure in the course of the transition from school to work, may then be reflected in the attitudes of the young people to those authority figures. One way of assessing such a possibility would be to examine in detail not only the attitudes of young people to teachers and supervisors but also to investigate their perceptions of the two roles, and to discover what they see as the important differences and similarities.

Alternatively, these differences in descriptions of teachers and supervisors may be a result simply of the short length of time for which the young workers had known the supervisors. Only nine months acquaintance may have been insufficient time for the young workers to get to know their supervisors personally. They may therefore have been more predisposed to describe supervisors in terms of professional characteristics, since their knowledge of them was largely restricted to the work environment. Whatever the explanation, there is certainly a need for more research in this area, and for attitudes to supervisors to be examined longitudinally to discover any changes which may occur during the process of transition and socialization to work.

The finding, that former Brookvale students were more favourable in attitudes to supervisors than former Woodbank pupils, is of interest, when taken in conjunction with the finding that they were also more favourable (on the same scales) in attitudes to teachers. It suggests that some socialization of attitudes to authority figures had taken place within the schools, and that the attitudes had persisted and had been carried over to the world of work. The same trend existed in attitudes to co-workers. Given that the kinds of jobs taken by the young people from the two schools did not differ in any significant way, it suggests that it was not differences between supervisors which produced the differences in attitudes. It appears more likely that attitudes to authority figures, engendered at school, persisted into working life. What this interpretation proposes is that attitudes to teachers at school become a prototype for attitudes to supervisors in the work organization. If this were so, we would expect, at an individual level, attitudes expressed towards teachers to be similar to attitudes expressed towards supervisors. Thus, Kevin, one of our sample, chose the items 'good to work for', and 'kind' as items to describe teachers, so we would expect him to choose the same items to describe supervisors. This possibility was investigated for all individuals in the survey over all items and it was found that there was not a significant correlation between items used to describe teachers and items used to describe supervisors (Appendix G). What we did find however, was that those individuals who had been most favourable in descriptions of teachers, were also the most favourable in descriptions of supervisors (though they did not necessarily use the same items to describe them). Similarly, those who had been most unfavourable in descriptions of teachers, were also those who were most unfavourable in descriptions of supervisors.

How do we explain this? It could be that there happened to be more individuals in Woodbank who generally described others in unfavourable terms. However, the differences between the pupils in the two schools were greater than would be expected by chance. We are therefore led to conclude that the schools had some effect in socialising attitudes to authority figures in organizations. An alternative explanation is that the less favourable attitudes to work held by former Woodbank pupils generally, also affected their attitudes to supervisors. Thus, it might be argued, that their more critical view of working life (produced possibly by their disapointment at having to take jobs of lower status than originally aimed for) produced a more jaundiced view of almost all aspects of their work, supervisors being only one amongst many of these aspects. The finding that attitudes to co-workers were less favourable among former Woodbank pupils would also be more consistent with this explanation and thus provides some support for it.

Whatever the explanation, it is apparent that some aspects of the organization and ethos of the schools affected subsequent attitudes to work and supervisors. The similarity of the catchment areas and jobs attained by pupils from the two schools makes explanations in terms of the schools themselves appear more likely. As Rutter has pointed out:

> '...individual actions or measures (within the schools) may combine to create a particular ethos, or set of values, attitudes and behaviours which will become characteristic of the school as a whole ...to an appreciable extent, children's behaviour and attitudes are shaped and influenced by their experiences at school and, in particular, by the qualities of the school as a social institution'.
> Rutter et al, 1979

Thus, our findings provide support for Rutter's position that secondary schools do have important influences on their pupils' behaviour and attainments. What they also suggest however, is that these influences on behaviour do not end when school life ends, but that the behaviours and attitudes shaped and influenced by experiences at school, and by the group influence resulting from the ethos of the school as a social institution, are likely to persist beyond school and into work life and may

affect not only attitudes to work itself, but even
social relationships within the world of work.

Chapter 9

JOB CHANGING

From the question 'what do you want to be when you grow up?' right through to careers education and advice in the latter years of secondary schooling, there appears to run an implicit assumption that most individuals are likely to hold the same job for the length of their working lives. As yet there is little knowledge about how effectively this assumption is inculcated and about how far it shapes school-children's perceptions of their future. What the available evidence does show is that it would be an unrealistic premise on which to start working life. A large proportion of school-leavers are likely to change jobs at least once within a short time period of taking up employment, and for the majority of them the decision to change jobs is a voluntary one.

Maizels (1970) found that, of the young people entering their third year of employment, half of the boys and three-fifths of the girls had had at least one other job since leaving school. Carter (1975) reported that in his study of school to work transition, during the first year of work, one-third of the sample had changed jobs. Five years later the figure had risen to nearly three-quarters. Cherry (1974) reported that in the National Child Development Study, 56.2% of the boys and 65.7% of the girls had changed jobs within three years of leaving school. The phenomenon is therefore one which is likely to characterise the lives of the majority of young school-leavers.

Much of the research work on job changing has tended to focus on the 'chronic job changer' and on young workers (Baxter, 1975; Cherry, 1976), and has attempted to discover what variables are related to persistent job changing. Baxter (1975) concluded that frequent job changing is linked with various forms of economic and social deprivation. Cherry (1976) found that, although persistent job-changing in the early years at work may indicate problems of personal adjustment, there was no evidence that it led to occupational problems. Indeed, Cherry concluded that

> 'a frequent change of employer appears to be a satisfactory and effective strategy for a young worker entering the labour market with a minimum of qualifications'.

Focussing on persistent job changing and attempting to find relationships with large numbers of variables tells us very little, however, about job changing during the transition from school to work. Given that many adolescents will change their jobs at least once soon after leaving school, it is worthwhile examining which particular groups, if any, are most likely to change jobs and to examine their reasons for so doing.

Job changing has been viewed in three different ways in the literature. Ginzberg et al (1951) argued that the change from school to work life is so great and so drastic that the school-leaver suffers a period of 'floundering' whilst adapting to the new norms, values and practices of working life. Theorists like Ginzberg (1951) and Super (1957) see vocational choice as a long process involving personal growth and developing awareness of one's self and one's environment. 'Floundering' is viewed as a characteristic of a stage of vocational development preceding vocational maturity and job-changing is seen as an overt indicator of floundering.

Miller and Form (1964) have suggested that job-changing is a constructive positive process which occurs during a period of trial and error on leaving school. The worker

> 'is trying to find and secure a job which satisfies his needs for expression for security and for recognition ...the trial work period commonly represents the personal struggles to find an occupation and a work plant where the worker feels these wants will be gratified'.

Similarly, Rodger (1961) proposes that job-changing is a 'planned procrastination' or 'systematic exploration' of the work environment resulting in the discovery, by young people, of the type of work suited to their capacities and inclinations . These ideas are based upon differentialist or matching models of occupational choice. The differentialists see individuals as having different abilities, interests and personalities, and view occupational choice as a process of matching these attributes with the requirements of available jobs.

A third explanation, proposed by Carter(1975), suggests that voluntary job-changing is a 'realistic reaction' on the part of young workers to the world of work. Carter sees job changing as

> 'but one aspect of the way in which workers address themselves to society ... even if they do change jobs, young workers are facing the situation which confronts them realistically'.

Voluntary job-changing, he suggests, is to be understood 'as a coming to terms with the world of work which is largely bereft of ... positive satisfaction'.

Each of these approaches is subject to criticisims. The floundering and trial-work explanations imply that job-changing, other than in the short term, is abnormal and this ignores the fact that sections of the economy require frequent labour turnover in order to be profitable e.g. building and tourist industries. Secondly, the trial work explanation is inevitably a post hoc explanation. Attributions of initial intent can only be made in the light of the eventual outcome. Thirdly, they ignore the wider social and economic contexts within which job-changing takes place. The theories have to take account of changing economic climates, but are not flexible enough to be predictive whatever the existing economic climate. It may well be, for example, that during periods of high unemployment in an economy, area or industry, job-changing will decrease since the worker will be reluctant to terminate employment whilst not being certain of gaining alternative employment. In times of high unemployment, young workers might be judged to have completed the transition process in terms of both 'floundering' and 'trial work' theories. In fact, job-changing would be constrained by the wider economic context.

Whilst attacking previous approaches to job-changing in adolescence, Carter (1975) says little about what job-changing is, and only appears to describe what job-changing is not (i.e. not a trial work period and not a period of floundering). Carter suggests that when they reach the age of 18 or 19 young people are beginning to consider the matter of settling down and are thinking 'in terms of marriage'. He concludes that this settling down period is a time when institutional support could be made available to advantage. All three theoretical explanations of job-change, however, fail to enable specific hypotheses arising from them to be empirically tested, and at the same time appear to be too generalised and vague to account for the many individual and situation-specific reasons for job-change given by young workers.

TOWARDS AN ALTERNATIVE MODEL OF JOB-CHANGING

Job-changing is one aspect of early working life which has received little attention in the past. Theoretical explanations have been vague and non-predictive and have achieved little, either in terms of our understanding of the phenomenon, or in application in training courses for careers guidance and teaching.

It is important to understand the reasons why job changing occurs if we are to identify it as a constructive or destructive element (or neither) in the transition process. If job-changing is a random and goal-less activity, produced by frustration with the realities of working life, then it could be taken as a sign of the need for careers guidance. If, on the other hand, job changing is a constructive testing or sampling of different work environments, preceding final occupational choice, then it is something perhaps to be encouraged. What theorists do is to propose models and theories to account for phenomena such as job-changing. These models and theories can then be examined to see how well they are supported by research evidence. We have already described three such models above.

It is possible to go some way towards an alternative, and hopefully better, model of job-changing based on the terminology and concepts of social exchange theory as originated and developed by Homans (1961). Social exchange theory posits a description of the way in which an individual assesses social situations and his or her consequent behaviour. Social situations are assessed in terms of the perception of the level of rewards and costs incurred by being a participant in one situation rather than any other possible situation. The individual's consequent behaviour will depend on his or her perception of the outcome of a particular situation relative to other possible situations: the overall profits he or she is making in a particular situation.

Thus, using the terms of the theory, each time an individual takes a job, costs are incurred and certain rewards result. The costs and rewards may be varied and may be along the same continua. For example, a well qualified young man may take a job as a coal miner, in a time of high unemployment, while he continues to search for work he considers more suitable. Among the costs for him, of taking such a job, may be unpleasant working conditions, boredom and unsociable hours. The rewards however, may include high pay, the chance of work in the short-term and the experience of industry, which may stand him in good stead in his potential career. In taking the job, the individual will assess the profits by subtracting the rewards from the costs. However, if the individual's stay in this occupation is prolonged beyond his initial expectations, he will reassess the situation, since the unpleasant working conditions of mining may begin to outweigh the benefit of high pay. Thus, it can be seen that rewards and costs are not static and that changing circumstances produce changes in perceived profits.

Thibaut and Kelly (1959) felt that simply looking at interaction in terms of outcomes would not be sufficient to determine when an individual would be satisfied with the results of an interaction. They introduced the term 'comparison level' to indicate how satisfied an individual will be with a certain outcome that he receives from an interaction. Borrowing this term and applying it again to the employment market, the comparison level would represent the outcome that an individual feels he or she deserves from a particular job, and its value will be influenced by all the outcomes known to the individual, either by direct experience or symbolically. If the profits of taking a particular job are above comparison level, the individual will be dissatisfied and not attracted to the job. Thus, the young man is likely to be less dissatisfied with his coalmining job if he knows there are many other equally well-qualified people who are unemployed and are unable even to secure jobs in the mining industry.

Thibaut and Kelly (1959) also introduced the concept of the individual's 'comparison level for alternatives'. Applying this to the employment market, the value of the comparison level for alternatives will depend on the profits that an individual thinks he can get from the best available alternative job. Thus, the comparison level for alternatives will determine whether or not an individual will stay in a particular job. If the profits of a particular job fall below the comparison level for alternatives the individual will be more likely to leave that job; if the profit is above the comparison level for alternatives, the individual will be more likely to remain in the job. Using these terms, it is possible to see that a person may remain in a job that he is very unhappy with, where the profit is below the comparison level, but above the comparison level for alternatives.

The usefulness of these concepts, in their application to employment and job-change among adolescents, is that we can include the wider social and economic context in the equation. Leaving a job in order to take an alternative job, which may not yet be guaranteed, can be examined to assess costs and rewards. One cost of leaving a job in a time of high unemployment may be the possibilty of unemployment for the individual. However, this may be partially offset by the possibility of unemployment benefits. Another cost might be the social stigma of unemployment. Thus, both leaving jobs and taking jobs can be examined in terms of anticipated profits.

How can this use of concepts from social exchange theory aid our understanding of voluntary job-changing amongst school-leavers? The existing theories of job-change amongst young workers, referred to earlier, have failed to take account of the wider social and economic context within which the change occurs. Utilising exchange theories it is possible to predict how these wider contexts will affect job-changing.

In previous studies of the transition from school to work (Maizels, 1970; Carter, 1975) it has been shown that adolescents change jobs quite frequently in their first years at work. Utilising the concepts described above it may be possible to explain this phenomenon in an empirically testable way. Before leaving school, most adolescents appear keen to leave school and start their working lives (Chapter 2). Undoubtedly, for many there is the feeling that beginning work is the beginning of adult life and independence, which involves freedom from the rules and restrictions of school. Working life may appear to be a new and glamorous change in status from school child to working adult. Indeed, many young workers view their new life styles in happy contrast to their old school lives (Chapter 2),

149

feeling that they are now more mature, independent and responsible. Society as a whole accords higher status to the adult than to the school child, and one characteristic of adulthood is having an occupation. Leaving school and starting work can therefore mean, for the adolescent, a major step towards acquiring adult status. Hence, the young workers may expect an increase in profits concomitant with their perception of increased status. At the same time, many find the quality of their life at work less satisfactory. Many school-leavers fail to get the jobs they had initially aimed for (Chapter 4) and one in four of the youngsters were either indifferent to, or disliked their jobs (Chapter 7).

Why should this be so? Studies in Britain have shown that adolescents have only limited ideas of what to take into account in weighing up the merits of different jobs, and are much in need of help, information and advice. The available evidence indicates that the majority of school-leavers are ill-prepared for working life, and their general level of job knowledge is low and based upon incomplete and often misleading information (Jahoda, 1952; Wilson, 1953; Carter, 1962; Jahoda and Chalmers, 1963; Roberts, 1968; Roberts, 1970; Maizels, 1970; Hayes, 1973; Hill and Scharff, 1976; Moor, 1976; Mack, 1977). In a review of research on organizational entry, Wanous (1977) concluded that the expectations of an organization, held by newcomers, are almost always inflated (except with regard to such factors as pay and working hours) and that the increasing experience in a new organization is associated with a less favourable view of it. Wanous also found that the use of realistic job previews in the recruitment of workers consistently reduced labour turnover for a wide variety of organizations. It would appear that inflated expectations are very common amongst school-leavers. Overall, the impression given in research reports is that 'school-leavers approaching work for the first time had little idea ...of what work would be like at all' (Hill and Scharff, 1976).

Careers guidance and teaching may well concentrate on giving young people a broad perspective of occupations and an understanding of methods of application, but a common complaint amongst the school-leavers in the present survey was that they did not have enough information about the content of jobs (Chapter 6). It is apparent that despite careers talks, work experience, careers lessons and all the modern media, young people have an incomplete impression of the reality of working life. Some appear unprepared for the boredom and stresses which are unhappy features of many jobs. Thus, their comparison levels on leaving school and starting work may well be unrealistically high. If this is the case and school-leavers' comparison levels for jobs are set too high one would predict that they would be more likely to change jobs early in their working lives. Their experience of the first job might produce low profits, and unrealistic comparison levels might lead them to believe that alternatives with higher profits exist, and are open to them. Job-changing may thus serve the function of setting young workers' comparison levels for jobs at a more realistic level. The reduction of job-change with time would then be expected to occur, since the expected profits of leaving jobs and beginning new jobs might increasingly be seen to be reduced.

Of course, the proposal that individuals enact significant life changes by taking account of possible costs and rewards is not in itself startling. What is important is to assert this cognitive dimension of job-change as a central functional factor, neglect of which incurs serious theoretical and applied problems. Attention to the psychological factors implicated in job-change is a necessary base for the formulation of an explanatory model of the interaction of the individual with the social context. A simple but essential first step in formulating such a model is to elicit subjective reports of the reasons for recent job changes from workers. It is also viable to ask people to describe the factors they would take, or had taken, into account in making a decision on whether or not to change jobs. For example, a reason for a job change might be higher wages offered elsewhere, while the factors taken into account might include the possibility of moving nearer (or further away from) friends or relatives etc. On an individual basis, these can be categorised as costs or rewards. Over a large number of individuals, it would be possible to estimate the relative salience of factors that people report taking into account in coming to a decision on job-change. This estimate is then open to empirical test, by field research and experiment, in order to investigate its applied utility.

A satisfactory account of the range and relative salience of factors taken into account, in job changes, leads at once to theoretically plausible and practically applicable predictions, which are again open to test. For example, it may be predicted that small adjustments to factors considered most salient would produce perceived changes in profits for the individual, where less salient factors would need to be altered considerably for any perceived change in profits to result. Determining the salience of factors for individuals might provide information on how best to attract young workers to areas of industry and the country where particular shortages existed, and away from areas of high unemployment.

Measurements might also be taken to evaluate how conscious the process of the evaluation of rewards and costs is in anticipation of job-change. Are there individual and personality differences in this respect? Is the degree of articulation of rewards and costs prior to job-change related to economic and personal satisfactions with outcome? Each of these questions promotes important methodological as well as applied considerations.

RESULTS

The number of job changes made by the young workers was checked at 9 months and 30 months into their working lives. By 30 months, nearly 40% of our sample had held more than one job, and over 25% of the sample reported that they were likely to be changing jobs in the near future. There was no significant relationship between the number of previous job changes and the reported likelihood of future job change. Those who had changed jobs in the past appeared to be no more or less likely to be changing employment in the near future, than those who had not changed jobs previously (Table 1).

In order to establish whether job changes appeared to be random we compared the observed frequency of changes with the frequency which might be expected by chance, calculated on the basis of the probability of only one change of job. There were no differences between the observed and the expected frequencies. This suggested that there was not a group of school-leavers who were persistently changing jobs. We found no significant relationship between job changing and sex, band, school, socio-economic background or number of exam passes at any stage of the study. Again, this suggested that no particular group was responsible for the job changing, but rather that it was a random phenomenon. However, one or two trends were apparent. The first was for the females to be more likely to change jobs than males - 44% of females had changed jobs at 30 months into their working lives, compared with only 31% of males. The second was for workers from the Woodbank 'B' band to change jobs more often than workers from the Woodbank 'A' band (52% of 'B' band compared with 37% of 'A' band).

These results are much in accord with what we would predict on the basis of the model of job changing proposed above. Firstly, we would expect job changing to be relatively random, in the sense that no one group accounts for most of the changes. We have argued that job changing is caused by school-leavers' comparison levels for jobs being too high. Research has shown that school-leavers have little idea of what work will be like and therefore, often expect too much of working life. If job changing is a result of this we would not expect it to be confined to one group, but to occur randomly over the whole sample. Secondly, our research suggests that females experience greater disillusionment and greater dissatisfaction than males on beginning working life (Chapter 7). Therefore, our model would predict that because their profits in jobs are low, that they would seek alternatives with higher profits - alternatives which they believe actually exist - in other words that they would change jobs more often than males. This is indeed what we found. A similar argument would apply to the differences we found between workers from the 'A' and 'B' bands of Woodbank.

An analysis of the jobs taken by school-leavers in our sample revealed that 31% of all job changes also involved a change of occupation. For example, Elizabeth P. left her job as a junior clerk and became a shop assistant, and we classified this as a change of occupation. There was a slight tendency for the males to change occupations more than the females, though this was not signigicant. There was no evidence that the young people either increased or decreased their socio-economic status as they changed jobs.

According to our model, the individuals who were most likely to judge their jobs as providing low profits, and who were most likely to believe that alternatives with higher profits existed, were those who did not attain their occupational aims. The data on job changing was therefore related to data on the degree of correspondence between stated occupational aims at the time of the first interview

TABLE 1 Number of job changes made by young workers at 9 months and 30 months after leaving school

NUMBER OF JOB CHANGES	9 MONTHS AFTER LEAVING SCHOOL	30 MONTHS AFTER LEAVING SCHOOL
None	76	88
1	16	33
2	4	18
3	1	2
4	0	3
No. of Respondents	97	144

TABLE 2 Reasons given by young workers for their changes in employment

CATEGORY	% OF TOTAL
Dislike of aspects of job, or dislike of job itself	17.4
Dissatisfaction with pay	15.9
Travelling difficulties	12.7
Boredom	12.7
Too little or no work (particularly piece workers)	7.9
Redundancy	7.9
Did not like employer, fellow workers	7.9
To try for better or preferred job	6.4
Dissatisfaction with prospects	6.4
Dismissal	4.8

Percentages represent the percentage of total responses which fall into each category

at school, and placement at the time of the final interview (Figure 1). The results showed that those who had not attained their occupational aims were significantly more likely to have changed jobs. In our terms, they were significantly more likely to have sought the alternatives with higher profits, which they believed existed.

This provides further support for our argument that job changing is not merely 'floundering', as Ginzberg *et al* (1951) have argued. Job changing appears to be a rational process in which the individual seeks to better his or her lot, believing that more profitable alternatives exist. Similarly, our findings would argue against Miller and Form's (1964) proposal that job changing is a constructive sampling of the available jobs, since it appeared that those who perceived themselves receiving relatively low profits (females, 'B' band, those who did not attain aims), were most likely to change. Job changing, amongst the young workers we interviewed, appeared to be a rational process, in which the individual assessed the rewards and costs of his or her current situation, against the profits of perceived alternatives.

Another interesting finding which emerges from examination of Table 2 is the apparent conservatism of many of the young workers. Whilst there was a degree of rational job changing taking place, half of those who did not achieve their aims, stayed in the first jobs they attained until at least thirty months after they had started work. Again this suggests that school leavers do not 'flounder' from one job to another, or constructively try out all the available opportunities.

Reasons for Job Changes
In examining the reasons given by young people for their changes of jobs, it is difficult to know whether or not the reasons given will be rationalisations disguising the real facts. For example, Wendy M. changed her job from a clerical worker in one organization to a clerical worker in another organization. She cited lack of promotion prospects, a clash of personalities with her supervisor, lack of facilities and bad working conditions as the reasons for this change. What we are unable to determine is whether a dismissal was ultimately the reason for the change. However, we are forced to accept the reasons given at face value since we could not check (both for practical and ethical reasons) with employers or work mates on the

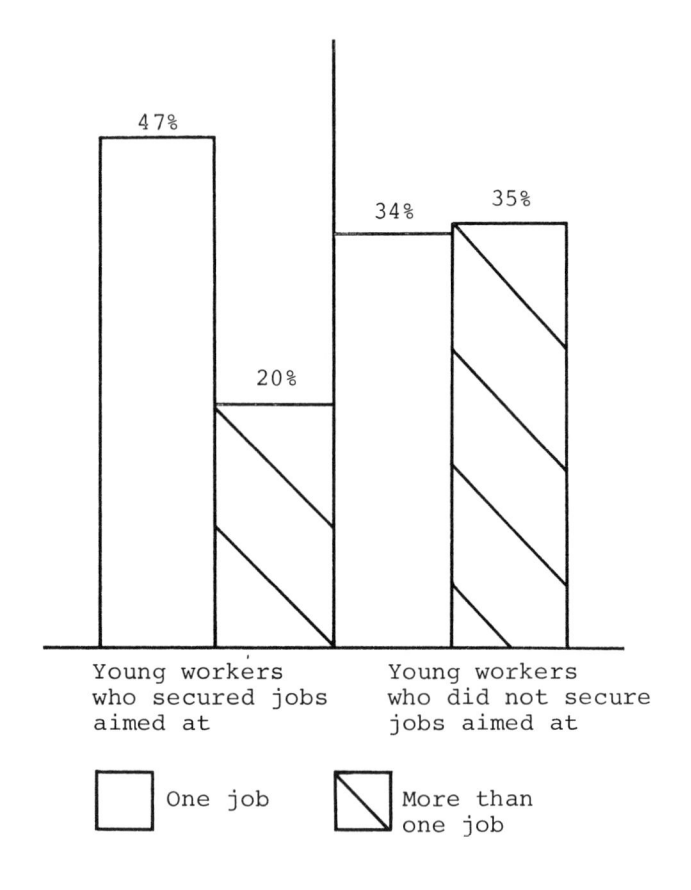

FIGURE 1 The relationship between job changing and degree of correspondence between occupational aims and attainments

validity of reasons given. With this proviso, the reasons given by young workers, for their job changes, are set out in Table 2. A variety of reasons was given e.g. Sheila D. changed jobs four times. The first and second job changes, when she was working as a machinist, were because there was too little work; the third time she changed from factory work which she found too heavy, and the fourth time she changed again from factory work because she didn't get on with the other women. Brian M. as another example, began his working life as a labourer but was soon made redundant. The next job he took as a labourer, he didn't like, and moved on to another labouring job. He was made redundant and for a fourth time took a temporary job as a labourer. Finally, he had a chance of a full time job as a storeman which he took. Overall, dislike of the job itself, dissatisfaction with pay, travelling difficulties and boredom were the reasons mentioned most often. The men were less likely than the women to cite too little or no work, or dislike of the job as reasons for job change; and women were less likely than men to be made redundant and much less likely to change because of the chance of a better or preferred job. These sex differences in reasons given, appear to reflect the differences in the kinds of jobs the men and women took, as well as the more limited alternative opportunities open to women.

CONCLUSIONS

Our results suggest that job-changing is a result of rational cognitive processes. The individual judges the profits arising from a particular job and, if they are found to be less than the expected profits of alternative jobs believed to be available, job-changing will be more likely to ensue. Since job changing is fairly frequent amongst young workers we would argue that their comparison levels, and comparison levels for alternatives, are set at an unrealistically high level.
Turning from these theoretical arguments to their applied considerations, if early job-changing were to prove to be a reaction to the realities of working life, and to have the effect of reducing comparison levels for alternatives, then it is possible that new approaches to careers teaching might usefully be employed. Hayes (1973) has suggested that considerably more attention should be devoted to giving information on the psycho-social

aspects of occupations, and Pumfrey and Warm(1972) have commented on the need for well-planned educational visits to improve the 'vocational maturity' of school-leavers. There is already much questioning of existing philosophies of careers education (Carter, 1975; Roberts, 1977) and at least one growing body of opinion holds that careers teachers and officers need to paint a more detailed and accurate picture of the quality and content of working life.

Obviously, not all job-changing is unnecessary. Within a society that is undergoing rapid economic and technological flux, job-change is almost an inevitability for the individual who wishes to remain in employment throughout his or her working life. It is important that the individual is prepared for employment change when it becomes necessary. From a broader economic perspective, the desirability of an informed and flexible work-force in such a society is self-evident. However, if a proportion of voluntary job-changing in working life is a result of incomplete or mistaken impressions of working life, it would seem useful to re-examine the processes by which these impressions are created and to attempt to alter them accordingly.

Chapter Ten

THE TRANSITION

'Since I left school and started work everything's better. I can buy my own clothes and I bought a stereo. At home, my mum treats me more like an adult now ...I go out when I want and they know I can be independent if I want to. I think I've got more respect for my family now as well. Being independent alters your feelings towards other people really. I think I've learned to get on with other people better ...I'm more sociable and friendly. I suppose I see things from a different point of view, I'm more sure of what I want, and I'm not afraid of people anymore. Things have changed a lot really'. Alan W.

In examining attitudes to schools and teachers, occupational choice, occupational attainments, entry into work, amongst the school-leavers in Woodbank and Brookvale, two trends consistently emerged. Firstly, students from the two schools differed in attitudes and experiences, and within Woodbank, there were sharp differences between 'A' band and 'B' band pupils. Secondly, the experience of the adolescent girls was generally very different from that of the boys. It could be that these differences we discovered are relatively unimportant in the lives of the individuals we talked to. Their views of themselves, their places in society, their hopes and expectations of the future, and their perspectives on the whole transition period, may be relatively unaffected. It may be that while individual aspects and stages of the transition differ for these groups, overall, the experience of adolescents leaving school and starting work is much the same. Alternatively, it might be that the differences we found are reflected in adolescents' views of the transition period as a whole, and that the adolescents' concepts of themselves in society are related to the kind of experiences they have during their transition from school to work.

For example, adolescent girls probably learn very quickly that society sees jobs for boys as more important than jobs for girls. Does this information lead to very different expectations of this period during adolescence, for girls and boys? We might expect some girls to be more home-centred than job-centred, modelling themselves on their mothers who fill the roles of house cleaner, food provider and care giver in the home. Others might be determined to have a good social life for a few years, making the most of their freedom prior to getting married and being tied by home and family. Questions such as these are important in the light of our increasing knowledge about the relationship between roles in society and mental health (e.g. Brown and Harris, 1978). What does leaving school and starting work mean in the lives of adolescents? Is it as exciting and rewarding as Alan's description above paints it? Or do some find the experience of beginning work a depressing and disappointing beginning to their adult lives?

In order to examine these issues, a number of more general questions were put to the young workers both at 9 months and 30 months after they had left school. These questions concerned the young workers' attitudes to society, the factors they considered most important in choosing jobs; effects of leaving school and starting work upon their lives in general, and their home lives in particular; their awareness of employment opportunities open to the opposite sex; their retrospective assessment of the most important features of leaving school and finding first jobs, and their expectations of life in the future.

RESULTS

1. Life Changes

Having left school and started work almost all of the young workers reported that going out to work had changed their lives considerably. Amongst the males, there appeared to be a strong feeling that changes in their lives were due partly to their meeting new people and learning to get on with them, but having money, independence and freedom were also frequently mentioned by them as important factors. Amongst the females, the most important factor in life changes resulting from their starting work, was reportedly having money (21% of all female responses). A large number also mentioned that they had grown up and become more mature and confident, and many mentioned that going out to work had made them more responsible. Other factors mentioned included a changed perspective of the world (e.g. 'I see things from a different point of view now, and I have a broader outlook'), going out more in the evenings, and having to get up earlier. The difference in emphasis, between boys and girls, upon the ways in which their lives had changed appeared to reflect the differences in development between the sexes during adolescence. Adolescent girls tend to be physiologically, emotionally and intellectually more advanced than boys and it may be that this is reflected in the ways in which they see their lives changing, consequent upon their starting work. In summary, the girls appeared to feel more grown up and responsible as a result of starting work, whereas the boys tended to emphasise independence, freedom and meeting new people as being the important changes in their lives.

2. Home-life Changes

The respondents were also asked whether starting work had changed their lives at home in any way. Whereas 68% of the boys reported that their home lives had changed in some way, only 45% of girls responded in a similar way and this difference was statistically significant (Figure 1). The boys tended to report that at home they were now treated more like adults, that they were respected, got on better with their parents and were generally treated as more responsible and mature. Only two of the girls reported that they were treated more like adults. The most significant way in which the home lives of the girls appeared to have changed, was as a result of their having money. Indeed only one female respondent reported getting on better with her parents since leaving school and starting work. These sex differences in changes in experiences at home appear to be centred upon the nature of the relationships between parents and their children. Going out to work appears to mark a major change in the parent-child relationship for boys, but much less so for girls. Thus, the boys appear to be treated more as adults as a result of going out to work. Girls' perceptions of the relationship reveal little change.

3. Expectations of the Future

At 9 months into working life, all of the young workers were asked what they hoped to be doing when they reached 25. Boys, in response to this question, mentioned jobs more frequently than anything else, whereas girls mentioned marriage the most frequently. 73 girls hoped to be married by age 25, compared with only 40 boys. Of the girls, 53 hoped to have children whilst 16 hoped that they would not have children. Of the girls who mentioned working after marriage, 28 intended to contine working and only 7 intended to stop work. This latter finding conforms with Hunt's (1968) survey result which showed that nearly three-quarters of girls in her sample, aged 16 and over and in full-time education, intended to continue working after marriage, and that nearly four-fifths of single women aged under 40 would continue to work if they got married.

In contrast,boys hopes were predominantly vocational and related chiefly to the jobs they hoped to be doing or to promotion that they hoped to get. As in Maizels' (1970) survey, hopes of marriage were expressed, but far fewer references were made to family life than among the girls, and these were generally secondary to vocational hopes.

These differences between the sexes may reflect a prevailing view in society. This is that adulthood for the male is generally marked by his entry into the world of work, whereas adulthood for the female appears to be contingent upon her marriage. The female's adult identity tends to be assumed upon marriage, whereas the male's adult identity is established by his beginning work. It is interesting that, in answer to these questions (particularly relating to expectations and hopes for the future), girls appeared to see their future identity more in terms of marriage and children, whereas boys tended to emphasise work and jobs more. This result is not confined to the present survey - the salience of marriage and motherhood for women, in future expectations, has been found to be paramount in previous studies. Veness (1962) found that marriage was mentioned by 94% of the girls and 67% of the boys in their life histories. Wilkins (1955) found that references to marriage dominated the replies of girls to questions relating to what they hoped to be doing by the age of 25. In Maizels' (1970) study, though references were also made to continuing in work until the arrival of children or, in some cases, to the return to work when children were older, two in three of the girls in her sample referred

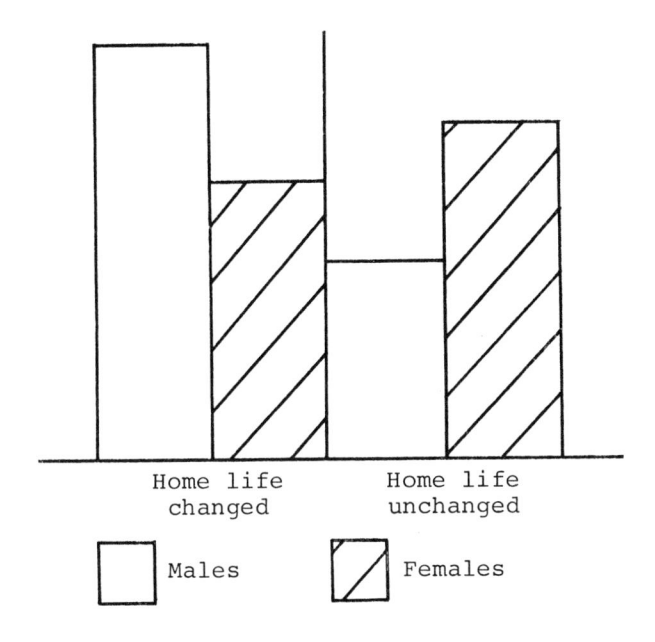

FIGURE 1　Differences in perceptions of changes in home life between males and females

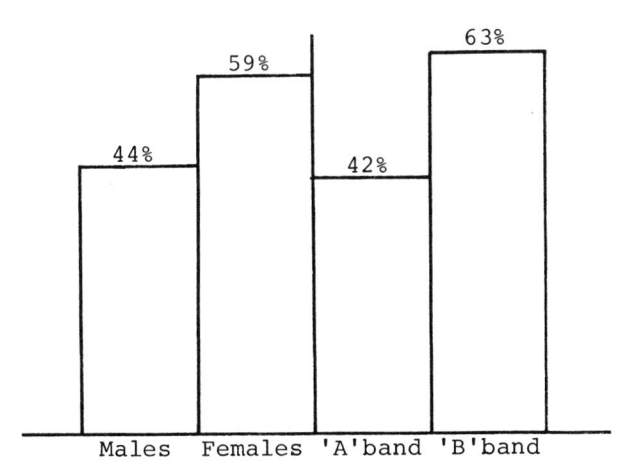

FIGURE 2　Average agreement with alienation statements: males, females, 'A' band and 'B' band workers

exclusively to their hopes for family life. There may well be therefore, a sense in which the independence, freedom and adult respect enjoyed by boys after their working lives begin, is, in the case of girls, contingent largely upon marriage. Such a broad generalisation may be inaccurate over all stratas of our society and possibly particularly in the case of better qualified girls leaving school or university. However, it suggests the subtle way in which society produces differential expectations in boys and girls and of the way in which girls are influenced towards accepting marriage as the institution within which they can realise an adult identity. Independence and freedom for the female would thus, paradoxically, be dependent upon her marrying and having children.

4. Alienation
It is possible from the measures we used to get some hint of the way in which the individuals in our survey saw themselves in relation to society generally. We were particularly interested in whether the differences between males and females, and between schools and bands within Woodbank, would be reflected in the responses to these measures. One set of questions we used dealt with the degree of alienation from society, felt by people within it. Srole (1956a, 1956b) has conceptualised this alienation or 'anomy' as a psychological state which refers to 'the individual's generalized, pervasive sense of 'self-to-others belongingness' at one extreme, compared with 'self-to-others distance' and 'self-to-others alienation at the other end of the continuum'. In other words, alienation describes the extent to which the individual feels separated from, and unsupported by others in society. To measure alienation or anomy, Srole devised a five item scale consisting of the following statements:

1. Nowadays a person has to live pretty much for today and let tomorrow take care of itself.
2. These days a person doesn't really know whom he can count on.
3. There's little use writing to public officials because often they aren't really interested in the problems of the average man.
4. In spite of what some people say, the lot of the average man is getting worse not better.

5. It's hardly fair to bring children into the world with the way things look for the future.

Subjects are asked to rate how strongly they agree or disagree with each of these statements, and an overall alienation score can be derived by adding together the number of statements with which the individual agrees. Thus, one can have an alienation score of zero, if one agrees with none of the statements, or an alienation score of five, if one agrees with all of them. Investigators who have administered the Srole scale to various samples in the United States, have uniformly reported that alienation is highest among minority and disadvantaged groups e.g. old people, the widowed, divorced and separated people, the less-educated, those with low incomes, and low prestige occupations, people experiencing downward social mobility, black people and immigrants.

From Figure 2 it can be seen that females appeared more alienated than the males and this was a highly significant finding. On statements 1 and 5 in particular, the differences between the sexes were very pronounced. Indeed, it is probable that the overall differences would have been even greater, had not statements 2,3 and 4 included specifically masculine references in the use of the words 'he' and 'man'. Females may have been less likely to agree with these statements because they contained these gender biases. Even so, on every statement, a greater proportion of females expressed agreement than did males. The average number of statements agreed with was 2.9 for females and 2.1 for males.

Why should these large differences in views of themselves in relation to society, exist between males and females? We have already documented how the initial experience of work was far more disappointing for women than for men, and how discrimination against women in the world of work is evident from the very beginning of their working lives. Such experiences must contribute to the degree of alienation felt by women. Moreover, the relative powerlessness of women in society may contribute to a feeling of alienation. Overall, female respondents appeared to have experienced less change than males in their lives since leaving school and starting work, and it has been argued that attainment of the adult freedom and independence referred to by males, as a consequence of beginning work, would generally come for females only when they had married. And yet, many would

165

view this as the exchange of one form of dependence (upon parents) for another (upon husband). If this is the case, then one would expect young married women to experience frustration and depression after marriage, since in many cases the release from dependence on parents and the increase in status achieved, might not compensate for the boredom and drudgery of the role of housewife and mother. Indeed, a number of authors have drawn attention to the high incidence of depression and anxiety amongst young married women, and have related this to the roles and status they are allotted in society (see in particular Gove, 1972; Brown and Harris, 1978; and Williams, 1979). If this is a valid interpretation of the data produced by our study, policy implications are apparent. It would be important for education to help adolescent girls establish their identity and social status outside of the institution of marriage. Perhaps what is needed is a real acknowledgement that work and other life activities (apart from marriage and motherhood) are important in the life of women. Obviously, this is influenced to a great extent by the breadth and social status of jobs available to women - a wider variety of jobs provides the opportunities for expression of identity which the current employment situation for adolescent girls hinders.

We also discovered sharp differences in the alienation scores of workers who were in the 'A' & 'B' bands of Woodbank school. Figure 2 shows how 'B' band students scored higher than 'A' band students on the alienation scale. On average, former 'A' band students agreed with only 2.1 of the alienation statements, whereas former 'B' band students agreed with 3.2. It is possible however, that those with fewer examination passes would be more alienated and that these band differences merely reflected differences between students of high and low ability. In order to examine this possibility we looked at the relationship between exam passes and agreement with alienation statements overall (Appendix I). Whilst there was a slight tendency for those with 7, 8 or 9 passes to agree with fewer statements than those with no examination passes, overall there was no significant statistical relationship. Once again it appeared that the system of banding employed at Woodbank school was exerting a significant and lasting influence on the lives, attitudes and experiences of the pupils who had passed through that system. A pessimistic but nevertheless plausible explanation, is that 'B' band students may have felt more powerless and alienated as a result of being categorised as less able and as failures, over a protracted period. While they may have responded to this by creating a sub-culture within the school, rejecting the formal values of the institution, they may still have felt alienated from the more powerful formal society within the school. This latter society was composed of the figures of authority and power, as well as of succeeding students. But even outside the school, they may still have felt more alienated on an individual basis in the wider society, and particularly since they did not have the support provided by the school sub-culture.

The fact that 'B' band students appeared to feel more alienated even after they had left school than did their 'A' band counterparts, cannot be explained entirely by factors related to employment. We investigated the relationship between the social class of job held and agreement with the alienation statements, and found no evidence of any significant relationship. These results lead to the conclusion that the differences in alienation between the bands are caused by the adverse social effects of the banding system and suggest that educationalists need to weigh very carefully the merits of such systems before employing them in educational institutions.

5. Sex Stereotyping in Jobs

In an attempt to assess perceptions of sex roles and sex stereotyping in jobs, subjects were asked what sort of jobs they would do if they were of the opposite sex. Of the 72 boys responding to this question, 42% said they would be secretaries. When asked the reason for their choice, boys' replies emphasised the job's desirability for girls - 'That's the best sort of job they can get' or 'That's what most of them go for, isn't it?'. The boys could not imagine doing the jobs themselves and several explained that girls were better at boring jobs. One boy suggested that all girls liked typing anyway. Of the boys, 10% said they would work in a shop if they were girls and a few had considered shopwork themselves, although none of them saw it as a first choice. Only 8 of the 72 boys said they would do the same job they preferred for themselves even if they were girls.

When girls were asked what they would do if they were boys, 23% out of the 80 subjects responding said that they would join the Forces. However, when asked about this possibility for themselves, many reported that their parents would not let them leave home. Others told of the discrimination in the Forces: that girls in the RAF were not allowed to fly, those in the Navy were not able to go to sea, and the girls in the Army had relatively little opportunity to travel. One girl wanted to be an airline pilot but had been unable to find an airline willing to train her. Mining and engineering were chosen by 28% of the girls as preferable opposite sex jobs. This large scale preference for mining and engineering is probably related to the status and glamour accorded these two occupations in the communities which we studied. Only four girls said that they would do the same job they preferred for themselves if they were boys.

Sex-role stereotyping, in relation to jobs, therefore appeared to be pervasive amongst both males and females. It appears that in traditional communities, such as those we studied, the introduction of equal opportunity legislation has had little impact upon patterns of occupational choice or patterns of employment.

6. Important Factors in Job Choices

In a previous study of the hopes for the future of fifth-form girls in London and Oxfordshire, Rauta and Hunt (1975) attempted to identify the factors considered important by girls in the choice of a job. The list of factors drawn up by Rauta and Hunt was also used in the present survey. The respondents were presented with cards with each factor written on one card e.g. 'A chance to travel', 'good money to begin with', 'a job you can forget when you go home'. They were asked to sort the cards into boxes to show how important each of these things was to them. The boxes were respectively marked: 'One of the most important things'; 'important, but not one of the most important'; 'not very important'; 'something I don't want at all'; 'don't know'. (Table 1).

Job security appeared to be the most important factor for the whole sample, as well as for groups within the sample (e.g. sexes, schools, bands, etc.). This replicated Rauta and Hunt's (1975) finding, that security was the most important factor in choice of job. Over half of the list of factors presented was perceived as important by 80% of the respondents. Girls and former 'B' band students tended to rate chances of promotion as much lower in importance than did males and 'A' band students, and this may again have reflected as much their perception of jobs open to them where promotion opportunities were available, as a negative attitude to promotion generally (see Chapter 6). The chance to make new friends appeared to be less important to former 'A' band students and males than to former 'B' band students and females. The psychosocial aspects of work can be important as a compensation for the lack of other intrinsic rewards associated with the job (such as status and higher wages), and our finding of increased importance to females and former 'B' band students of social factors in jobs may be related to this fact.

7. Leaving School and Starting Work

At 2½ years after leaving school the young workers were asked to write their feelings on what they remembered about leaving school and finding their first jobs. Most reported that they were pleased to leave school, though some felt sad about leaving old friends. Generally, the young workers reported that they were excited at the prospect of starting work and pleased and relieved to have found jobs when so many young people were out of work. At the same time, very few felt that they would ever get the best job they could reasonably imagine themselves getting, even given good luck and their own hard work. They were also asked for any comments which they thought might help with the research. Almost all of these comments concerned recommendations for better methods of careers teaching:

> 'I think job experience should be done at an earlier age and pupils should be sent to a place where they think there is the type of work they would like to do, so that they can find out at an early stage that it's not all they expected it to be, and not send them just where work was available.'
> 'The school careers officer was only there to give you information on work around, they did not supply information on vacancies.'
> 'Careers teachers should be more in touch with industry.'
> 'In the careers lesson the teacher is drilling it into their heads that all they are fit for is factory work.'
> 'Children should be encouraged by teachers if they really are keen on a career, whatever it may be; I found people very disheartening when they told me "no way".'
> 'Children should start making decisions about their future much earlier and so gain enough

TABLE 1 The importance of different factors in choice of jobs

ITEM	%
A secure job	98
Friendly people to work with	89
Variety of work	88
A chance to make new friends	87
A chance to make money later on	87
A good training scheme	85
A chance to learn new things	85
A job where I know what is expected of me	85
Good chances of promotion	85
Good money to begin with	70
Plenty of responsibility	62
A job close to home	55
Time off to go to college	54
A job you can forget when you go home	50
A chance to travel	45
Being left to work on your own	44

Percentages represent percentages of respondents indicating each item as being an important or one of the most important factors in choice of job

knowledge about a job before jumping into something they find they can't get out of.'
'The careers service were helpful in telling you about available jobs, but they didn't give you enough information about the jobs and what it involved.'
'I think there should be a lot of work experience before leaving school, giving a chance to see what they would like to do, and seeing the difference in all kinds of jobs.'
' I think the lessons could be adapted more, e.g. domestic housewiring, car maintenance, how to sign on the dole.'
'Visits to industry from school helped a lot.'
'Careers officers should steer you towards the job that one wants to do and not take the first job that's available or what they think will suit that person.'
'The teachers took us on trips to factories and the higher people on trips to offices. The teacher himself split us up into two groups who he thought was good enough for the jobs and I myself was taken to a factory when I wanted an office job.'
'Give children more freedom for looking for jobs when they're still at school.'

In retrospect the young workers appeared to feel that there was a need for more information about jobs, more real-life experiences of work prior to choosing jobs and a need for more attention to be paid to the individual needs and aspirations of young people leaving school, regardless of how clever they were.

SUMMARY

Questions concerning general attitudes, hopes and expectations of young people during the period of transition from school to work revealed that, for many, their lives appeared to have undergone a significant change. Boys felt they had acquired freedom and independence and were pleased to be meeting new people and having their own money. The girls emphasised how the transition had been marked for them by a growing maturity and confidence. At home, boys saw themselves as being treated with more respect and as being more responsible and mature. Significantly more boys than girls reported that their home lives had changed as a result of their leaving school and starting work. This difference appeared to centre on the nature of the relationship with their parents. This perhaps reflects the prevailing view in society that adulthood for the male is contingent upon beginning working life, whereas for females, marriage marks the beginning of adult 'freedom and independence'.

More females than males mentioned marriage in descriptions of expectations for the future, whereas boys' hopes for the future were predominantly vocational. Girls also appeared to feel significantly more alienated from society and to feel less able to change things. This finding is significant when considered in relation to research on sex roles and mental health, and it is suggested that it is important for schools to help females to consider establishing their social identity in spheres other than marriage.

There were significant differences between former 'A' band and former 'B' band pupils in alienation scores, the latter scoring significantly higher. These differences did not appear to be related either to educational ability (as measured by examination passes), or to the social class of the jobs held by the young workers. It therefore appears that the adverse social effects of the banding system employed at Woodbank extended into the working lives of those young people who had passed through the system.

Questions on sex-role stereotyping of jobs revealed a significant degree of stereotyping, but external forces, such as jobs available to one sex and the traditional nature of the two communities, appeared to exert a strong influence in strengthening this stereotyping.

The importance of different factors in determining job choice was also assessed. Job security appeared to be the most important factor for all groups, with factors such as 'chance to make money later on', 'good training scheme' and 'a chance to learn new things' also appearing prominently. Girls and former 'B' band students tended to rate chances of promotion as a less important factor, and social aspects of jobs as more important factors.

Finally, general comments elicited from respondents suggested a concern with methods of careers teaching and a perceived need for more information about jobs and more work experience schemes.

Chapter Eleven

CONCLUSIONS

'Adolescence, in the Western world at least, is probably the second busiest period of development, second only to infancy in the number of critical events that can occur. Perhaps the most important event during adolescence is the choice of a role by which the individual can enter society as an independent figure, contributing to, as well as taking from, the larger social group. Choosing a role very much defines one's status in society. Since role choice is very much a process of self-definition, adolescence may be described as a time of self-discovery or self-creation.' (Bower, 1980)

The results of this study have highlighted at least two major influences upon the adolescent's role and status. The first is the influence of the school and the second is the influence of gender. In addition, our findings have implications for the methods and practice of careers guidance and teaching.

SCHOOL ORGANIZATION AND ETHOS

Adolescents who attended Woodbank were less positive, and more negative, in their attitudes to both their teachers and their schools than were adolescents who attended Brookvale. They were also likely to choose jobs of relatively high status. Having left school and started work, former Woodbank (the banded school) pupils appeared to be less happy and settled in their jobs and to find their work less interesting than former Brookvale pupils. Finally, former pupils of Woodbank school were consistently less positive in evaluations of supervisors than were former Brookvale pupils. These results suggest that some characteristics, or combination of features of the schools we studied had a significant effect upon pupils' attitudes to teachers and schools, their job choices and their attitudes to work and supervisors.

In speculating upon the causal factors responsible for the differences we found, one stands out above all others - academic streaming. When attitudes to teachers and schools were examined within Woodbank (the streamed school), we found that adolescents from the 'A' band (the higher academic stream) were significantly more positive in attitudes to teachers than were adolescents from the lower band. Perhaps part of the explanation for the differences between the schools lies in the effects of streaming. It is a well-established finding that the organization of schools into academic streams profoundly affects social relations within the schools (Hargreaves, 1967; King, 1969). Pupils in the higher academic streams interact together more and develop a more academic orientation. They have more commitment to the academic values of the school and staff and tend to be critical of those who reject the establishment norms. Pupils in lower streams also have to achieve 'status' and need to achieve respect in the eyes of peers. Consequently, those who do not achieve scholastically may seek achievement elsewhere and react against the school system as a whole. The development of counter-cultures in schools, along these lines, has been vividly portrayed by Hargreaves (1967) and Willis (1978).

However, the process may not involve a subculture which is even actively anti-school, as Rutter has pointed out (Rutter et al, 1979). Rather, there may be the formation of peer groups within a school which are merely indifferent to academic success since there is little chance for them to achieve success. Consequently their goals must be located in other spheres of activity (e.g. being 'one of the lads'):

> 'For children who are unlikely to gain any examination passes, there may be few advantages in being part of an institution in which one of the explicit objectives is academic success and in which the norm is scholastic commitment. If the intake to any school consists of a very high proportion of less able children, there will be an increased tendency for the formation of non-academic social groups indifferent or opposed to academic success.

> ...(This will) increase the likelihood of
> conflict between teachers and pupils...'
> (Rutter et al, 1979)

How much more pronounced would these effects be in a school where even the teaching staff, on the basis of qualifications, were assigned to teach 'A' band or 'B' band pupils? Such was the situation in the streamed school in the present survey and it does seem likely that, in these circumstances, effects of streaming would be accentuated. At the same time, it would be unwise to draw firm conclusions on the basis of the results of one study involving only two schools, since these schools may represent only exceptions to a general trend. However, the results do provide sufficient data to warrant further investigations of the questions raised, particularly since differences in educational ability between the streams, was consistently not an explanation for the differences in attitudes and experiences.

A second possible causal factor is related to academic streaming and this is the extent of the emphasis which is placed generally upon academic achievement within the school. Woodbank school, before becoming a comprehensive school, had been a grammar school and many of the teachers had stayed on at Woodbank when it became a comprehensive school. Emphasis on academic achievement in the 'A' band was high. 'A' band pupils were expected to take 'O' level GCE examinations and the schools also had a growing number of sixth-formers studying for 'A' level examinations. The better qualified teachers tended to be assigned to the 'A' band and the less qualified teachers were 'relegated' to teaching 'B' band children. It should be pointed out that whilst this was not a formally declared policy within the school, it appeared to be almost inevitably the way teachers and classes were matched.

Brookvale school had formerly been a secondary modern school before it became a comprehensive. Consequently, many of the teachers working at Brookvale were the original secondary modern teachers. Within Brookvale, classes were organised broadly along mixed ability lines and none of the pupils took 'O' level examinations, the headmaster preferring to concentrate on preparation for CSE examinations. There was no sixth form in Brookvale and there were no students preparing for 'A' level examinations.

The two schools differed sharply, therefore, on a number of characteristics which are related to academic values. These differences may have combined to produce different attitudes and expectations amongst the pupils attending the two schools. For example, pupils attending Woodbank may have been led to believe that working life represented the rewards for perseverance at school, and may consequently have been disappointed in their experience. This may then have led them to be more critical of their jobs, their work and their supervisors. It would seem that the effects of banding could also be heightened in schools with high expectations for their students. With an increasing emphasis on examinations and qualifications, students are led to expect a good job when they leave school. These expectations, in the present survey, were found to be unrealistic in relation to the available job opportunities.

Whatever the explanations for the differences in job choices and attitudes to teachers, schools, work and supervisors, the implications are apparent. The possibility that some features of schools can have an effect upon pupils' attitudes to work after they have left school and started work is one which merits further investigation. Understanding of employee attitudes and behaviour must require attention to be paid to the expectations of employees on their entry into work, and in so far as schools influence these expectations, an examination of the effects of school processes and ethos prefaces an understanding of attitudes and behaviour in the world of work.

SEX DIFFERENCES IN TRANSITION FROM SCHOOL TO WORK

The adolescent girls in the present study made more negative statements and fewer positive statements about teachers than did the boys. Paradoxically, the girls appeared to like school more than the boys and were less keen to leave. Having left school, they were then less happy at work than were the boys. Girls were less likely than boys to receive formal training for work and less time was spent introducing girls to firms and work. Females were also unlikely to describe their jobs as interesting; unlikely to express strong positive attitudes to work, and more likely to express strong negative attitudes than males early in working life; girls tended not to be considering promotion; were less settled, were lower paid, and were more often paid on a piecework system.

Discussion of these sex differences cannot

profitably be undertaken without reference to sex role expectations in childhood, and particularly in adolescence, since as Ireson (1978) has forcefully argued, socialization, particularly socialization into a female sex role, negatively affects girls' achievement patterns and occupational aspirations. Two traditional sex role values are of particular importance in understanding processes and experiences of transition from school to work for females: (1) the woman's place is in the home, bringing up a family; and (2) the male is primarily responsible for providing economic support and pursuing a career. Forces of socialization not only affect the individual adolescent female's behaviour, they also affect the expectations and attitudes of teachers, careers officers and employers and so can directly influence the advice they give to girls (Schlossberg and Pietrofesa, 1973; Friedersdorf, 1970).

The forces of socialization during the early years are usually those of the family and especially parents. Later, added to these, are teachers, friends and the media (particularly television). In adolescence, all these agents of socialization remain important, but added to these are peers and the school peer culture. These agents tend to socialise males and females into traditional sex roles. Females are expected to be dependent, warm, emotionally expressive, sensitive, submissive and to pursue feminine goals such as attractiveness, marriage, motherhood and domesticity. Males, by contrast, are traditionally expected to be aggressive, confident, independent and competitive. Those who violate existing sex-role expectations may be rejected or exposed to riducule. Such social sanctions are powerful enough to ensure that most people conform, to a greater or lesser extent, to the stereotypes.

How does the socialization of sex roles affect the processes of transition from school to work? Firstly, we found sex differences in attitudes to teachers, girls being significantly more unfavourable than boys in their evaluations of their teachers. How do such differences arise? Preadolescent girls' academic achievements are higher than those of boys, and girls perform better and are more likely than boys to work to their full ability in school (Emmett, 1954; Lavin, 1965). But early in adolescence, a proportion of girls begin to decline in achievement (Shaw and McCuen, 1960; Campbell, 1973). Ireson (1978) and Douvan

(1979) have argued that during adolescence the female experiences a critical role conflict and this conflict may be partly responsible for the differences we discovered. Throughout childhood girls are socialised to be dependent and, at the same time, to be competitive, individualistic and achievement-orientated in school. Studies of adolescent self-concept have indicated that sex-role identity is central to self definition during adolescence and that sex-linked interests and goals dominate adolescents' behaviour. Consequently, achievement-orientated, competitive, individualistic behaviour is less important for female sex-role identity, since it is not sex-linked, nor is it central to sex role stereotypes of females. Coleman's (1961) study of adolescent sub-culture demonstrated that status in the adolescent world depended upon meeting sex-linked criteria: for boys this was athletic performance and for girls social leadership. Intelligence was especially devalued among middle class girls: popular, good-looking girls were much more likely than intelligent girls to be wanted as friends and to be respected as role models. As they moved through adolescent years, boys came to value academic achievement more and girls valued academic attainments less - even in the final year of school.

Such social-psychological processes may therefore be the underlying cause of the sex differences in adolescence in attitudes to teachers which we discovered. The girls' changing attitudes to academic achievement may have been reflected in their attitudes to teachers. The paradoxical finding that girls were less keen than boys to leave school may be explained by the fact that boys had a more positive inducement to leave school in the form of work opportunities. Occupational aims, hopes and expectations played a much less important part in the plans of girls for the future.

Attitudes to work, of the girls in our sample, tended generally to be less positive than those of boys. The simplest and most obvious explanation is that the conditions of employment and work for the girls in the present survey were objectively worse than those enjoyed by the boys. The girls were more often paid according to a piecework system (where availability of work, as well as work produced, governed the size of the week's wages), were unlikely to work overtime and tended not to have any additional benefits from their work. They were also less likely than boys to receive formal training for their jobs, or to be shown around the firm in

which they worked. On an international scale there is much evidence of similar discrimination against women in industry.
    Even prior to leaving school, however, there is evidence that males are prepared better for the world of work than girls. Boys' vocational aspirations are usually well-developed by middle adolescence, while girls hold less articulated occupational aims and are less well-informed about the educational requirements for the jobs they choose (Douvan, 1979). Ireson (1978) has referred also to the pattern of limitation evident in girls' occupational development. Girls indicate much less varied occupational aims and both sexes consider fewer occupations open to women. During the adolescent years when girls' academic interests decline, the range of occupations chosen by girls also narrows. The social pressures on adolescent girls to aspire to sex-appropriate occupations and to relinquish ambitious, achievement-orientated career plans are undoubtedly strong. Within the present survey there was evidence that girls making inappropriate sex-role choices were pressured into changing their choices by both institutional agents, such as careers officers, as well as by family and friends. Behaviour, such as striving to achieve, which is not seen as compatible with the role of wife and mother, is thus discouraged. Television further contributes to this socialization process. Children's television programmes and advertisements portray sex roles in rigid stereotyped ways (Sternglanz and Serbin, 1974). Dominick (1979) has also reported that while the number of women shown on American television as housewives and housekeepers has declined from the 1950's to the present, the make-up of the television labour force has been inconsistent with the real-life employment patterns of women in the United States of America. More are being shown in the service category of occupations, but the majority of these are portrayed as detectives and police officers. Dominick's results show that women are under-represented in TV programmes, and provide abundant evidence that stereotyping still exists on a large scale in American television. There is little reason to doubt that the same is true of British television protrayal of women's occupational roles.
    The effect of all these pressures is to socialise women to restrict their job choices more than men (there are also rules and laws which restrict certain occupations to men only e.g.mining,

179

priesthood, service at sea in the Royal Navy) and to lower their aspirations. There was ample evidence of sex-role stereotyping in our survey. It is unlikely therefore, that women will express their full potential in their work if, in some way, they have lowered their occupational aims. This might well produce a more disaffected attitude to work amongst women than men. The female role of worker is devalued relative to that of the male, and even where both partners in a marriage are working, the female occupation is seen as secondary in importance to that of the male. In our society the male role of worker is generally valued above that of the female role of worker, and this message is communicated in both overt and covert ways to females and must undoubtedly have effects upon women's attitudes to work. The fact that so few females received training for their jobs relative to males in the present study bespeaks something of the jobs themselves as well as of employer's attitudes to the jobs suitable for the female work force. This is also communicated to the female worker and must again affect attitudes to work.

Overall, the period of transition wrought more changes in the lives of males and females in the present study. The males felt that they had acquired freedom and independence and saw themselves as treated with more respect and as more responsible and mature. The females felt that they were more mature and confident since leaving school, but fewer females than males reported that their home lives had changed. For males, adulthood appears to be marked by the entry to work, whereas for females marriage and motherhood appear to represent adult status (see Chapter 10). It appears that the major tasks society expects a woman to carry out are to get married and to have children. This is the norm which is communicated to women, and full adult status appears to be contingent upon its fulfilment. The male's task appears to be mainly to secure and keep full-time employment. Consequently, more females than males in this survey mentioned marriage in their plans for the future whereas males' hopes were predominantly vocational. Locksley and Douvan (1978) similarly found differences between male and female adolescents in expectations of the future. They found that girls who thought they would marry relatively early conditioned their occupational plans accordingly, while those who aimed at high status occupations tended to postpone marriage and motherhood in their concepts of the future. The males did not show this co-ordination between job and family plans.

Finally, the girls in the present survey appeared to feel significantly more alienated from society than the males and appeared to feel less able to change things. We have discussed this finding in relation to research on sex roles and mental health (Chapter 10), arguing that females' exchange of dependence upon parents for dependence upon husband, in return for adult status, can create frustration and depression after marriage. We have also argued that it is important for females to establish their social identity in spheres of life other than marriage and at least equally with males in the occupational world.

CAREERS EDUCATION AND GUIDANCE

In recent years careers education in Britain has been influenced to a great extent by developmental theories of vocational guidance. As a result, careers officers tend to see themselves more in a counselling role, and as less obligated to local employers. The new training programmes for careers officers and teachers emphasise a psychological counselling approach, training advisers to work with individuals in a supportive and relatively non-directive role.

In proposing a new theory of occupational choice, Kenneth Roberts (1976) expresses serious reservations about developmental theories in vocational guidance. He suggests that individuals are rarely involved in meaningful job choices but are limited by their qualifications and by the range of available jobs. As an alternative to developmental theories of vocational development which stress personal growth and development (Super, 1957; Ginzberg, 1972), Roberts proposes a theory of opportunity structure. He states: 'Careers can be regarded as developing into patterns dictated by the opportunity structures to which individuals are exposed, first in education and subsequently in employment, whilst individuals' ambitions, in turn, can be treated as reflecting the influence of the structures through which they pass' (1976, p. 142).

In the present study it was possible to explore some of those issues since the careers teacher in Woodbank was a vigorous proponent of the developmental approach to careers guidance. In Brookvale, by contrast, the careers teacher had a more traditional approach to his job, seeing it as one of finding jobs and placing his students in work. An examination of initial occupational choices of the school leavers in the two schools revealed that young people from Woodbank aimed at jobs of higher status than those from Brookvale. We have already discussed how the emphasis on academic attainment and the system of banding employed at Woodbank could have produced heightened expectations of their prospects in the world of work among Woodbank pupils. It may be, however, that the relatively high aims of these pupils were raised also by the careers teaching employed at Woodbank. A developmental approach perhaps encourages students to be more imaginative and ambitious in their occupational aims. Students from Brookvale were less likely to aim high in choosing occupations and this lower target setting may derive from the methods used by the careers teacher at this school, whose advice to students was closely tied to the local opportunity structure. The students from Brookvale might therefore have seen their occupational futures in more restricted and traditional ways as a result of their exposure to the differentialist techniques of careers teaching.

Students from Brookvale school eventually attained jobs of slightly (though non-significantly) higher status than they had aimed for, but Woodbank pupils (from both 'A' and 'B' bands) attained jobs of lower status than they had aimed at. Furthermore, socio-economic status of jobs aimed at proved to be higher amongst those who did not achieve their aims, but there were no differences in status of jobs obtained between those attaining original aims and those not. These results suggest that pupils from Brookvale set themselves 'realistic' aims which they were able to fulfil, whereas Woodbank pupils had to modify their unrealistically high targets. One of the criticisms of the developmental approach to careers teaching is that it fails to deal with the realities of employment. When there is high unemployment, many individuals with the appropriate qualifications cannot find jobs equal to their abilities and qualifications. Their expectations are thwarted and they are forced to take relatively low level jobs or have no jobs at all. This experience, while demoralising at any age, has the potential for profoundly affecting young people's attitudes towards work and society. Our findings suggest that this may be precisely what happens since pupils from Woodbank had generally less favourable attitudes to work.

If the results of the study are related in isolation to the methods of careers teaching used in the two schools, our findings can be seen to provide clear support for the line of argument followed by Kenneth Roberts (1976). Our results imply that far from aiding students in the transition from school to work, a developmental approach merely aggravates and exacerbates the difficulties faced by adolescents in adjusting to the opportunity structures which exist in the world of work. The developmental approach ignores the reality of high levels of unemployment, of the boredom, stress and drudgery of work, and of the situational factors which prevent adolescents from seeking work wherever it may be. By ignoring the reality of present society, where the possibility of implementing a self concept and moving in the direction of self actualisation through work exists only for a minority, careers guidance officers and teachers may be doing a disservice. The good intentions and optimism embodied in the developmental approach should not be sufficient reasons in themselves to pursue a particular method of counselling. Whilst it is hard to dismiss a philosophy which is essentially positive and humanistic, and which encourages individual initiative and self-reliance, it is folly to pursue a theory which is still unproven in practice and which appears ill-equipped to cope with the realities of the present (and the short-term future) in which unemployment is high, and where young people leaving school are often hardest hit. The argument that the developmental approach is only pertinent to educationally more able youngsters who are able to make genuine career decisions, also appears to be valid, since it is they who achieve the higher status jobs and who are therefore more likely to have jobs where the implementation of a self concept is a possibility and not a dream. Jobs in which self concepts may be expanded, where awareness of one's self in relation to society is broadened, and where growth towards an ideal concept of self can be nurtured, simply do not exist for a large proportion of youngsters in modern industrialised society. This should not be seen as an argument for restricting the developmental approach only to those most able adolescents, since such élitism would only amplify the social divisions within schools.

The problem lies not in the ideals themselves, for encouraging self-awareness in young people, and encouraging them to be themselves and to implement their self concepts and ideals in their activities, are surely policies which many educationalists would favour. Using such an approach at the end of a school life during which an emphasis on examination passes may have outweighed considerations of broader learning, and prior to the adolescent's entry into the world of work would seem to be over-optimistic in the face of the realities. School life involves learning facts, concepts and ways of thinking about academic and applied subjects. Education is not aimed at fostering self-awareness or existential experiences, and using a few careers lessons to fulfill this function is rather like nurturing a distorted fully grown oak tree with a watering can.

However, it is not possible to judge the effects of careers teaching in the two schools in isolation from other factors. We have no way of partialling out effects of banding from the effects of careers teaching. But whatever the explanation, our results provide considerable support for Roberts' position. Either ambitions and attitudes to work were shaped by local opportunity structures and by the educational institutions through which individuals had passed, or the consequences of developmental approaches to careers guidance were to aggravate the difficulties of adjustment faced by the young people in the study.

At the same time, we would caution against following the advice of Roberts to those involved with school leavers, that they should seek 'to reconcile individuals to job opportunities, many of which allow little scope for personal development' Roberts, 1975). Such an approach ignores the dynamics of a changing society, for to discourage rising expectations is (to an extent) to encourge stagnation and apathy, for the role conflict and frustration of aspirations and expectations (again within limits) can be a form of constructive conflict within society as a whole. Young people who protest about the nature of their work may be a force for useful change in society. If we attempt to shape acceptance of monotony, drudgery and danger in young people, we only perpetuate a poor quality of working life. Encouraging adolescents to examine their working conditions can lead to constructive attacks upon working conditions generally and upon the individual's quality of working life in particular. Reconciling young people to their lot, no matter how unpleasant, is also contrary to the interests of those who aim high and achieve their goals (like, for example, Daniel E. who became a first division footballer), and those who attain jobs better than they might otherwise have hoped for. Furthermore, such an approach might have the effect of strengthening existing divisions in society. It implies that educationally less able youngsters should be persuaded to accept that their working lives must necessarily be less satisfying or more stressful than the working lives of those who are more educationally able. The political questions underlying such an implication are serious, not least because more is now known about the very real physical and mental stress associated with different kinds of working life (see for a review, Warr and Wall, 1975). The suggestion that young people should be reconciled to existing opportunities is one which should be seriously questioned.

There are serious weaknesses in both the developmental approach and in Roberts' suggestions. What about the traditional differentialist method of fitting 'round pegs in round holes'? Such a method places a large burden of responsibility on the individual who advises the adolescent. It requires him or her to accurately judge the abilities and interests of the young person, and to correctly match them with the best available occupation. It is doubtful whether people could be successfully trained to carry out such a task efficiently, particularly because so many variables affect individual occupational choice (Chapter 3). Furthermore the importance of the task demands a particularly high level of efficiency since advice given can have such far-reaching effects upon the adolescent's life. The ideas that careers teachers and officers can match individuals with jobs, that they should be involved in reconciling adolescents to their lot, and that they should work to deepen the individual's knowledge of himself and his environment, all incorporate a strongly paternalistic element. They suggest that there is an accepted expertise which can help individuals to arrive at the best occupational choices for them, and which can help individuals through the transition period. We would argue against this for two reasons. Firstly, the transition from school to work remains an ill-understood period in adolescent life, and secondly, there are still no generally accepted criteria for evaluating the effectiveness of careers guidance (Watts and Kidd, 1978). Undoubtedly, many different approaches have value and it would be unwise to discard an approach to careers education without determining what aspects, if any, are useful. But the results of the present survey indicate strongly the need of school leavers from both the schools (and therefore the need appears to be independent of careers teaching style) for more information about the world of work upon which they could base job choices. At all stages of the survey, the young people repeatedly referred to the lack of detailed information available to them about specific jobs. They also mentioned the need for more information on wages, taxes and the intricacies of pay slips, and there was an overwhelming expression of need for more information about jobs and working life generally. If school leavers indicate that they have too little information available upon which to base their decision-making, the implications for careers teaching are apparent.

The need for realistic job previews (as opposed to distorted positive previews) has been illustrated in the past (Weitz, 1957; Wanous, 1977) and we have argued it is particularly important for adolescents to be given a more accurate picture of the world of work if the transition is to be made easier and smoother for them. Almost all (98%) of the adolescents in our survey thought that work experience visits would be a good way of providing the information they needed, and a number of studies have indicated the value of such visits (Pumfrey and Warm, 1972; Hayes, 1973; Youthaid, 1979). Certainly, where work experience is provided, attitudes of pupils to their last year of school are far more favourable and there is every reason to suppose that the provision of work experience visits for school leavers would go some way towards dispelling the anxiety and bewilderment experienced by adolescents in their first days of work. Such programmes require co-operation between local industries, careers guidance officers and schools, but co-operation between these institutions is surely to the advantage of all concerned and students can be given the information they require in addition to detailed information about local job opportunities and patterns of employment. In this way, adolescents can make their own informed decisions more easily, and the activities of careers teachers either in deepening individuals' self awareness or in reconciling individuals to the realities of the world of work may become less crucial. This effectively gives young people the responsibility and the ability to make their own decision on a choice which is likely to have lasting and far-reaching effects upon their happiness and quality of life. Ultimately, it is they who should be making that decision, and suggestions that adults can better decide for them are based on the presumption that adolescents are not capable of making this kind of important decision. It is perhaps a telling example of the way in which the adolescent's transition is as confusing for adults as it is for adolescents. In this case, a major life decision for which only the adolescent can take responsibility, is shaped by adults who see adolescents as incapable of making that decision alone. The important point is that adolescents are no longer children and have reached the stage in life where they must make their own decisions. The task of those involved in teaching and guidance, should surely be to give them as much factual information as possible, in order that their final decisions are informed.

Perhaps of equal importance is the need for schools to provide students with advice on coping with unemployment. We have not dealt with this problem in the study, largely because most of the young people in our survey were in full-time employment. Also, we set out with the aims of studying the transition from school to work, and not the transition from school to unemployment. Nevertheless, it is an area which requires the most urgent consideration and practical suggestions for alleviating the difficulties of the individuals affected. It may be that widespread social change is required before many of the problems we have discussed can be solved. Sex discrimination in industry is unlikely to disappear overnight and the stigma of unemployment is likely to remain for some time as an additional burden upon those who cannot find work. However, the fact that large scale social change is required is not a sufficient reason to ignore the problems. Unemployment amongst young people is widespread and schools are the obvious institutions within which they can be prepared to avoid or cope with unemployment.

There are many processes involved in the transition of the school leaver to working life and they remain ill-understood. The effect of educational institutions upon ambitions and attitudes has been suggested by the results of the present study and our work needs to be extended to cover more schools of differing organizational structures, and which incorporate varying styles of careers teaching. But considering transition from school to work in isolation from research on adolescence generally we believe has been one of the faults of previous work in this area. Super, for example, has drawn attention to the concept of the self in the process of occupational choice, and yet whilst there exists a body of research work on the development of self in adolescence (for reviews see Burns, 1979; Wilson, 1979), researchers and theoreticians have failed to link these areas to examine changes in self concept in the transition period amongst adolescents of both sexes. Similarly, research has provided information about peer group formation, the developmental significance of peer group relationships and the influence of peer groups in adolescence, but no attention has been paid to the dramatic change in the structure of peer groups which can occur when adolescents leave school and start work. In general, the area of adolescence has received remarkably little research attention in Britain apart from the important studies conducted by Coleman (Coleman, 1974; Coleman, 1979; Coleman et al, 1977a; Coleman et al, 1977b). Certainly, far more of current theory and research on the psychology of adolescence needs to be incorporated into attempts to comprehend the period of transition from school to work.

Throughout this book we have referred to the paucity of research work carried out in Britain on the transition from school to work and one area in particular appears to demand attention: the entry into working life of young people is still poorly understood despite the fact that beginning work probably represents the most salient developmental point in the transition period from school child to working adult. This is an area where social psychological studies, drawing upon existing methodologies and theoretical approaches to socialization might be invaluable. The application of such research might be beneficial to both young workers and to those who employ them or who seek to successfully integrate them into organizations.

Probably the most disturbing aspect of this research has been the discovery of the consistently unfavourable experiences of females leaving school and starting work. Whilst this aspect is obviously a reflection of more general sex discrimination in our society, we were surprised by its extent, particularly in training provided by firms for employees. The enormity of this problem is best judged by the degree of alienation reported by the girls in this survey (relative to the boys), and the very real effects their experiences in leaving school and starting work must have upon self esteem and mental health. There are few easy solutions to pervasive social problems and it is only to be hoped that current changes in attitudes to the female role will continue so that females leaving school may have equal opportunities for self expression in the world of work. In this context there is also a persisting need for schools to be satisfied that differences in the curriculum between the sexes do not unfairly and unnecessarily militate against the personal development or the career prospects of girls(Department of Education and Science, 1975).

Finally, we were aware at all stages of this study of a reluctance in the schools for too much time to be expended on teaching 'careers' at the expense of examined subjects and there is undoubtedly a need for all involved in education to be made aware of the importance of the transition period. We may conclude that schools can do much to influence expectations and attitudes to work and that schools and management in industry can do much to ease the way of young people into the world of work. We would therefore hope that the results of the present study will be examined in detail, and extended in future studies, in order that the potential of educational and employing institutions may become more fully understood.

APPENDIX A

ATTITUDES OF SCHOOL LEAVERS TO TEACHERS AND SCHOOLS

TABLE 1 Percentages of respondents choosing positive items to describe teachers

ITEMS	% OF RESPONDENTS (PRESENT SURVEY)	% OF RESPONDENTS (MAIZELS,1970)
Professional:		
Know their job	33.3	48.5
Explains things clearly	37.4	44.9
Encourage me	37.4	40.6
Efficient	17.2	23.0
Listen to what I say	23.0	31.5
Praise me when I do well	16.7	31.2
Good to work for	20.7	24.6
Clever	19.0	16.1
Full of ideas	16.1	13.9
Personal:		
Helpful	70.7	57.9
Fair	62.6	43.3
Treat me like a human being	35.1	33.9
Pleasant	46.6	31.5
Reliable	21.3	17.9
Sincere	5.7	12.7
Kind	20.1	17.0
Confident	9.2	10.0
Always keep promises	7.5	10.9
TOTAL number of responses	174	330

Pearson Product Moment Correlation Coefficient:

$r = 0.86$; $df = 16$; $p = \leq 0.001$

TABLE 2 Percentages of Respondents choosing negative items to describe teachers

ITEMS	% Of RESPONDENTS (present survey)	% Of RESPONDENTS (Maizels, 1970)
Professional:		
Strict	25.3	35.5
Have favourites	46.0	36.4
You never know where you are with them	19.5	17.9
Expect too much	18.4	14.6
Don't seem interested	17.2	8.8
Muddled	0.6	15.8
Personal:		
Sarcastic	24.7	22.4
Moody	25.3	20.0
Too old	14.4	16.1
Too young	10.9	14.6
Nagging	17.2	15.8
Frightening	6.9	8.8
Interfering	5.2	2.7
TOTAL number of respondents	174	330

Pearson Product Moment Correlation Coefficient:
r = 0.08; df = 11   p = < 0.001

191

TABLE 3 Percentages of respondents in Bands 'A' and 'B' choosing items to describe teachers

	POSITIVE ITEMS			NEGATIVE ITEMS	
ITEM	'A' Band	'B' Band	Item	'A' Band	'B' Band
Professional:			Professional:		
1.	34.6	25.0	1.	17.3	27.8
2.	36.5	30.6	2.	53.8	36.1
3.	46.2	25.0	3.	21.2	27.8
4.	21.2	8.3	4.	19.2	27.8
5.	21.2	8.3	5.	23.1	16.7
6.	15.4	13.9	6.	1.9	0.0
7.	21.2	13.9	$\bar{x} =$	22.7	25.7
8.	15.4	8.3	Personal:		
9.	3.8	25.0	7.	42.3	27.8
$\bar{x} =$	23.9	20.8	8.	28.8	27.8
Personal:			9.	9.6	22.2
10.	67.3	61.1	10.	11.5	11.1
11.	69.2	47.2	11.	13.5	27.8
12.	38.5	25.0	12.	7.7	11.1
13.	44.2	50.0	13.	5.8	5.6
14.	23.1	16.7	$\bar{x} =$	24.8	24.3
15.	11.5	2.8			
16.	13.5	13.9	N =	52	38
17.	9.6	5.6			
18.	1.9	11.1	t= 0.3926; df=12; N.S.		
$\bar{x} =$	26.3	25.4			

N =   52   38

t = 2.328; df = 17; p = <0.05

TABLE 4   Percentage of items chosen by pupils to describe schools

FAVOURABLE ITEMS	PRESENT SURVEY	MAIZELS, 1970
Offers a good standard of education	51.7	60.9
Up to date	48.3	51.7
Helps everyone to do their best	36.8	43.0
Has a good reputation	46.6	40.0
Efficient	32.2	33.0
Friendly	46.0	47.0
Just the right size	36.8	33.0
Easy going	19.0	20.4
	$r= 0.9$; $p=<0.01$	

UNFAVOURABLE ITEMS		
A lot of lessons seem a waste of time	43.1	25.5
Not enough practical training	27.0	17.0
Only interested in the brainy ones	19.0	17.0
Too set in its ideas	5.7	14.2
Needs fresh people at the top	12.1	6.1
Strict about time-keeping	29.9	45.5
Too many rules and regulations	21.3	20.9
Too strict	2.3	19.7
Not enough discipline	21.0	17.0
Too big	16.1	10.9
	$r= 0.5$; N.S.	
N =	174	330

APPENDIX B

OCCUPATIONAL CHOICE

TABLE 1 Status of school-leavers' occupational choices

SOCIO ECONOMIC STATUS OF OCCUPATIONAL CHOICE		WOODBANK SCHOOL	BROOKVALE SCHOOL
High	1	5	1
	2	26	7
	3	27	33
	4	17	30
Low	5	11	12

Chi^2 = 17.6; df = 3; p = < 0.001

Chi^2 for Band x Status of Choice = 19.97; df = 1; p = < 0.001

Chi^2 for 'A' Band x Brookvales' Status of Choice = 41.73; df = 2; p = < 0.0001

Chi^2 for number of jobs mentioned x Bands = 5.13; df = 3; p = < 0.05

APPENDIX C

FINDING JOBS AND SOURCES OF HELP

TABLE 1 Length of time taken by school-leavers to secure jobs as a function of examination passes

NUMBER OF EXAM PASSES	WHEN LEFT SCHOOL	WITHIN 1 MONTH OF LEAVING	GREATER THAN 1 MONTH
0 - 2	22	11	33
3 - 6	16	10	26
6 +	14	20	34
TOTAL	52	41	93

Chi^2 = 4.84; df = 4; p = < 0.09 (not significant)

Band by length of time taken to secure first job:
Chi^2 = 9.70; df = 1; p = < 0.01

Number of job applications made by school-leavers before they secured their first jobs as a function of number of examination passes:
Chi^2 = 7.59 df = 2: p = < 0.05

Band by number of job applications before securing first job:
Chi^2 = 9.88; df = 2; p = < 0.01

TABLE 2 Helpfulness of classes or qualifications in getting jobs

RESPONSE CATEGORY	% OF RESPONDENTS	'A' BAND	'B' BAND
Yes, definitely	27.1	9	4
Yes, maybe	11.5	2	3
Uncertain	3.1	1	1
No	58.3	6	20
N= 96	100.0	N= 18	N= 28

Chi^2 = 6.57; df = 1; p = < 0.02

Helpfulness of classes or qualifications in getting jobs as a function of number of examination passes:
Chi^2 = 2.4; df = 2 ; N.S.

APPENDIX D

AIMS AND ATTAINMENTS

Socio-economic status of jobs attained as a function of examination passes:
$Chi^2 = 20.61$; df = 4; $p = <0.01$

Band differences within Woodbank school in the status of jobs attained:
$Chi^2 = 24.6$; df = 1; $p = <0.001$

Chi^2 for differences in status between aims and attainments (Woodbank pupils):
$Chi^2 = 10.18$; df = 3; $p = <0.02$

Chi^2 for differences in status between aims and attainments (Brookvale pupils):
$Chi^2 = 2.46$; df = 3; N.S.

TABLE 1 The relationship of status of jobs aimed at and attainment or non-attainment of occupational aims

SOCIO-ECONOMIC STATUS OF JOBS AIMED AT		ATTAINMENT OF AIMS	NON-ATTAINMENT OF AIMS
High	1	1	4
	2	7	16
	3	25	29
	4	20	17
Low	5	15	3
N =		68	69

$Chi^2 = 13.5$; df = 3; $p = <0.005$

APPENDIX E

ENTRY INTO WORK

TABLE 1 The relationship between number of examination passes and the length of time for which school-leavers were willing to train for a job:

	NUMBER OF EXAMINATION PASSES		
	0	1 - 5	MORE THAN 5
Less than 6 months	6	5	0
6 months to 3 years	25	14	10
As long as necessary	34	12	10

$Chi^2 = 4.84$; df = 4; N.S.

The relationship between type of training received and sex of school-leaver (see Table 2, Chapter 6).

$Chi^2 = 28.3$; df = 3; $p = <0.001$

APPENDIX F

ATTITUDES TO WORK

The relationship between attitudes to work and sex of respondent at 9 months into working life (see Table 1, Chapter 7).
$Chi^2 = 10.43$; df = 3; p = < 0.02

The relationship between attitudes to work and time into working life (see Table 1, Chapter 7).
$Chi^2 = 7.82$; df = 3; p = < 0.05

The relationship between attitudes to work and sex of respondent at 30 months into working life (see Table 1, Chapter 7).
$Chi^2 = 0.64$; df = 2; Not significant

The relationship between perceived job interest and sex of respondent (see Table 3, Chapter 7).
$Chi^2 = 13.94$; df = 3; p = < 0.01

TABLE 1 Aspects of jobs most liked and most disliked by respondents:

LIKES		DISLIKES	
CATEGORY	% RESPONSES	CATEGORY	% RESPONSES
Social	49	Aspects of job itself	19
Job interest	27	Pay, conditions, hours	16
Economic	10	Bosses or co-workers	16
Variety	9	Menial tasks	13
Supervision	5	Boredom	10
		Getting up early	7
TOTAL	100	Training	5
		Travel	4
		Nothing	10
		TOTAL	100

TABLE 2 Interest characteristics of their jobs as described by respondents:

CATEGORY	% RESPONDENTS
Positive interest	
Interesting	48.4
Chance to use initiative	31.6
Have to concentrate	28.4
Interesting product/service	28.4
Varied	45.3
Uses brains	18.9
Skilled	18.9
Negative interest	
Too routine	7.4
Not enough skill	5.3
Monotonous	6.3
Boring	10.5
N =	95

Pearson's r (Present survey results and Maizels)
= 0.88; df = 9; p = <0.001

Differences between schools on positive interest items:
t = 3.72; df = 7; p = <0.01

Differences between sexes on positive interest items (ignoring items 3 and 4).
t = 3.06; df = 4; p = <0.05

TABLE 3 Demand and physical characteristics of their jobs as described by respondents

CATEGORY	% OF RESPONDENTS
Demand	
Keeps you busy	60.0
Pause when you want to	34.7
Responsible	40.0
Difficult	15.8
Competitive	10.5
Needs nimble fingers	8.4
Physical	
Mainly indoors	34.7
Dirty	30.5
A lot of moving about	26.3
Clean	24.2
Mainly sitting	18.9
Noisy	18.9
Badly organised	6.3
Too heavy	5.3
N =	95

Differences between bands on demand items:
t = 4.557; df = 5; $p = < 0.01$

Differences between bands on physical items:
t = 2.846; df = 7; $p = < 0.05$

TABLE 4 Social and status characteristics of jobs described by respondents

CATEGORY	% OF RESPONDENTS
Work with a good crowd	65.3
A steady job	32.6
Teaching me something useful	38.9
Work with own age group	25.3
Offers promotion prospects	36.8
Well paid	38.9
N =	95

Pearson's r (Present survey results and Maizels)
= 0.79; df = 4; N.S.

Differences between schools:
t = 3.59; df = 5; p = < 0.02

The relationship between sex of respondent and methods of payment (Table 4, Chapter 7).
Chi^2 = 19.74; df = 2; p = < 0.001

The relationship between sex of respondent and levels of weekly pay (Table 5, Chapter 7).
Chi^2 = 6.71; df = 2; p = < 0.04

The relationship between school attended and anticipated changes of job (Table 6, Chapter 7).
Chi^2 = 10.81; df = 2; p = < 0.01

The relationship between sex of respondent and interest in promotion or changing jobs (Table 7, Chapter 7).
Chi^2 = 6.82; df = 1; p = < 0.01

The relationship between sex of respondent and interest in promotion or changing jobs at place of work.
Chi^2 = 6.82; df = 1; p = < 0.01

APPENDIX G

ATTITUDES TO SUPERVISORS

The relationship between school attended and attitudes to co-workers (Table 1, Chapter 8).
$Chi^2 = 5.43$; df = 1; p = < 0.02

The relationship between school attended and attitudes to supervisors (Table 1, Chapter 8).
$Chi^2 = 4.89$; df = 1; p = < 0.05

TABLE 1 Percentages of respondents choosing positive items to describe supervisors

ITEMS	% OF RESPONDENTS (present survey)
Professional	
Knows his/her job	61.3
Good to work under	52.7
Explains things clearly	47.3
Encourages me	40.9
Listens to me	39.8
Praises me when I do well	36.6
Efficient	23.7
Clever	21.5
Full of ideas	20.4
Personal	
Helpful	55.9
Fair	48.4
Treats me like a human being	38.7
Considerate	37.6
Pleasant	36.6
Reliable	32.3
Kind	28.0
Confident	14.0
Sincere	8.6
Always keeps promises	8.6
TOTAL number of respondents	93

Pearson Product Moment Correlation Coefficients:
Present Survey and Maizels r=+0.90; df=17; p=< 0.001
Attitudes to Supervisors and Teachers
    r=+0.73; df=16; p= < 0.001
Attitudes to Supervisors (Maizels) and teachers
    r=+0.78; df=16; p= < 0.001

TABLE 2 Percentages of respondents choosing negative items to describe supervisors:

ITEMS	% OF RESPONDENTS (present survey)
Professional	
Has favourites	15.1
Expects too much	14.0
Strict	8.6
Muddled	6.5
Doesn't seem interested	5.4
Personal	
Moody	20.4
Sarcastic	14.0
Nagging	11.8
Interfering	5.4
Too old	4.3
Too young	3.2
Frightening	2.2
TOTAL number of respondents	93

Pearson Product Moment Correlation Coefficients:
Present Survey and Maizels: $r=+0.63$; $df=10$; $p=<0.05$
Attitudes to supervisors
  and teachers: $r=+0.68$; $df=10$; $p=<0.05$
Maizels and attitudes to
  teachers: $r=+0.27$; $df=10$; N.S.

The percentages reported by Maizels in her study, and the percentages choosing items to describe teachers at school, are included to enable comparisons. The correlations between attitudes to supervisors and attitudes to teachers, and between Maizels' findings and the present findings in relation to attitudes to supervisors, have also been calculated.

Turning firstly to positive items chosen to describe supervisors, a high positive correlation was found between the results of the present survey and the results of Maizels' survey. Similarly, there was high positive correlation between the percentages of respondents choosing items to describe teachers and supervisors. A comparison of the two correlations revealed no significant

203

difference ($z = 1.514$; $p = 0.06$). However, the percentages of respondents choosing positive items were significantly larger than the percentages in Maizels' survey ($t = 5.38$; $df = 18$; $p = <0.001$). Similarly, the percentages choosing positive items to describe supervisors were significantly greater than the percentages choosing positive items to describe teachers in the earlier interviews ($t = 2.18$; $df = 17$; $p = <0.05$). This latter difference was most striking when positive items relating to professional characteristics were compared ($t = 4.05$; $df = 8$; $p = <0.01$). A comparison of negative items chosen to describe teachers and supervisors on the checklist revealed that the respondents were significantly less negative in evaluations of supervisors than they were in evaluations of teachers ($t = 3.19$; $df = 11$; $p = <0.01$).

TABLE 3 Percentages of positive and negative items chosen by respondents to describe supervisors

	POSITIVE	NEGATIVE	TOTAL
Professional	38.2 (24.5)	10.3 (21.2)	28.1 (23.2)
Personal	32.4 (31.0)	8.8 (14.9)	21.8 (24.0)
TOTAL	34.4 (27.8)	9.2 (17.8)	24.6 (23.6)

Percentages =

$$\frac{\text{Total number of responses within a category}}{\text{Total number of possible responses within a category}} \times 100$$

Figures in brackets represent percentages of items chosen to describe supervisors

The correlation between items chosen to describe favourable characteristics in teachers and supervisors, across all respondents:

Pearson's r = 0.049; Number of cases = 102; N.S.

The correlation between items chosen to describe unfavourable characteristics in teachers and supervisors, across all respondents:

Pearson's r = 0.07; Number of cases = 102; N.S.

The correlation of individuals who were most favourable in descriptions of teachers with those who were most favourable in descriptions of supervisors:

Spearman's r = 0.25; Number of cases = 102; p=0.007

The correlation of individuals who were most unfavourable in descriptions of teachers with those who were most unfavourable in descriptions of supervisors:

Spearman's r = 0.18; Number of cases = 102; p=< 0.05

APPENDIX H

JOB CHANGING

The relationship between number of job changes and length of time into working life:

$Chi^2 = 9.58; df = 2; p = <0.01$

The relationship between job changing and the correspondence between occupational aims and attainments:

$Chi^2 = 6.1; df = 1; p = <0.02$

APPENDIX I

THE TRANSITION

The relationship between perception of home life changes and sex of respondent (Figure 1, Chapter 9).
$Chi^2 = 4.33$; df = 1; p = < 0.05

TABLE 1 Percentages of respondents agreeing with alienation statements

ALIENATION STATEMENTS	MALES	FEMALES	'A' Band	'B' Band
1.	56.8*	76.4	43.5**	85.7
2.	56.8	67.3	60.9	64.3
3.	43.2	50.9	47.8	50.0
4.	43.2*	56.4	34.8	60.7
5.	20.5	43.6	21.7	53.6
NUMBER OF RESPONDENTS	44	55	23	28

* Difference significant at p = < 0.05
** Difference significant at p = < 0.01

Alienation scores of respondents:
Chi^2 Males and Females   = 13.82; df = 3; p = < 0.005
Chi^2 'A' Band and 'B' Band = 8.56; df = 1; p = < 0.01

The relationship between number of examination passes and agreement with alienation statements:

$Chi^2 = 4.62$; df = 3; Not significant

The relationship between social class of job held and agreement with alienation statements:

$Chi^2 = 17.7$; df = 20; Not significant

BIBLIOGRAPHY

Allen, E.A. (1961) Attitudes to school and teachers in a secondary modern school, British Journal of Educational Psychology, 31, 106-109

Arvidson, G.L. (1956) Some factors influencing the achievement of first-year secondary modern children, Unpublished PhD thesis, University of London

Ashton, D.N. (1973) The transition from school to work: Notes on the development of different frames of reference among young male workers, Sociological Review, 21, 101-125

Ashton, D.N. and Field, D. (1976), Young Workers, Hutchinson, London

Barker Lunn, J.C. (1970) Streaming in the Primary School, N.F.E.R., Slough

Barker Lunn, J.C. (1971) Social Class, Attitudes and Achievement, N.F.E.R., Slough

Baxter, J.L. (1975) The chronic job changer: A study of youth unemployment, Social and Economic Administration, 9, 3, 184-206

Bower, T.G.R. (1980) Human Development, W.H.Freeman, San Francisco

Bray, D.W., Campbell, R.J., and Grant, D.L. (1974) Formative Years in Business, Wiley, New York

Brown, G.W. and Harris, T. (1978) Social Origins of Depression: A Study of Psychiatric Disorder in Women, Tavistock, London

Buehler, C. (1933) Der Menschiche Lebenslauf als Psychologische Problem, Herzel, Leipzig

Burns, R.B. (1979) The Self Concept: Theory, Measurement, Development, and Behaviour, Longman, London

Bush, R.N. (1942) A Study of student-teacher relationships, Journal of Educational Research, 35, 645-656

Campbell, P. (1973) Feminine intellectual decline during adolescence, Unpublished PhD thesis, Syracuse University

Carter, M.P. (1962) Home, School and Work, Pergamon, Oxford

Carter, M.P. (1975) Teenage workers: A second chance at 18, In Brannen, P. (Ed) Entering the World of Work: Some Sociological Perspectives, H.M.S.O., London

Cherry, N.M. (1974) A study of job stability in a national survey of young workers, Unpublished M.Phil. thesis, University of London

Cherry, N.M. (1974) Do careers officers give good advice? British Journal of Guidance and

Counselling, 2, 1, 27-40
Cherry, N.M. (1976) Persistent job changing - Is it a problem? Journal of Occupational Psychology 49, 203-221
Child, D. (1973) Psychology and the Teacher, Holt Rinehart and Winston, London
Clarke, A.M. and Clarke, A.D.B. (1976) Early Experience: Myth and Evidence, Open Books, London
Coleman, J.C. (1974) Relationships in Adolescence, Routledge and Kegan Paul, London
Coleman, J.C. (1979) The School Years: Current issues in the Socialization of Young People, Methuen, London
Coleman, J.C., George, R. and Holt, C. (1977a) Adolescents and their parents: A study of attitudes, Journal of Genetic Psychology, 130, 239-245
Coleman, J.C., Herzberg, J. and Morris, M. (1977b), Identity in adolescence: present and future self-concepts, Journal of Youth and Adolescence, 6, 63-75
Coleman, J.S. (1961) The Adolescent Society, The Free Press, New York
Crites, J.O. (1969) Vocational Psychology, McGraw Hill, New York
Crowther Report (1959) Central Advisory Council for Education, 15-18, H.M.S.O., London
Daws, P. (1977) Are Careers Education programmes in Secondary schools a waste of time? - A reply to Roberts, British Journal of Guidance and Counselling, 5, 1, 10-18
DeFleur, M.L. (1964) Occupational roles as portrayed on TV., Public Opinion Quarterly, 28, 1, 57-74
DeGroat, A.F. and Thompson, G.G. (1949) A study of the distribution of teacher approval and disapproval amongst sixth-grade pupils, Journal of Experimental Education, 18, 57-75
Department of Education and Science (1975) Curricular Differences for Boys and Girls Education Survey 21, H.M.S.O., London
Dominick, J.R. (1979) The portrayal of women in prime time 1953-1977, Sex Roles, 5, 4, 405-411
Douvan, E. (1979) Sex role learning, In Coleman, J.C. (Ed), The School Years: Current Issues in the Socialization of Young People, Methuen, London
Emmett, E. (1954) Secondary Modern and Grammar School performance predicted by tests given in Primary Schools, British Journal of Educational Psychology, 24, 91-98
Equal Opportunities Commission (1978) 2nd Annual

Report 1977, H.M.S.O., London
Ferri, E. (1971) *Streaming: Two Years Later - A Follow-up Study of a Group of Pupils who attended Streamed and Non-streamed Junior Schools*, N.F.E.R., Slough
Finlayson, D.J. (1973) Measuring school climate, *Trends in Education*, April, 19-27
Friedersdorf, N. (1970) A comparative study of counsellor attitudes toward the further educational and vocational plans of high school girls, *Dissertation Abstracts International*, 30, 4220-4221
Ginzberg, E. (1972) Toward a theory of occupational choice: A restatement, *Vocational Guidance Quarterly*, 20, 169-176
Ginzberg, E., Ginsburg, S.W., Axelrod, S. and Herma, J.L. (1951) *Occupational Choice: An Approach to a General Theory*, Columbia University Press, Columbia
Gove, W.R. (1972) The relationship between sex roles, marital status and mental illness, *Social Forces*, 51, 34-44
Gray, H.L. (1975) On starting a new job, *Journal of Occupational Psychology*, 48, 33-37
Handyside, J.D. (1961) Satisfactions and aspirations, *Occupational Psychology*, 35, 4
Hargreaves, D.H. (1967) *Social Relations in a Secondary School*, Routledge and Kegan Paul, London
Havighurst, R.J. (1953) *Human Development and Education*, Longren, New York
Hayes, J. (1973) Work experience and the perception of occupations, *Occupational Psychology*, 47, 121-129
Hayes, J. and Hopson, B. (1971) *Careers Education and Guidance*, Heinemann, London
Hill, J.M.M. and Scharff, D.E. (1976) *Between Two Worlds*, Careers Consultants Limited, London
Holland, J.L. (1966) *The Psychology of Vocational Choice: A Theory of Personality Types and Environmental Models*, Ginn, New York
Homans, G.C. (1961) *Social Behaviour: Its Elementary Forms*, Harcourt, Brace and World, New York
Hoult, P.P. and Smith, M.C. (1978) Age and sex differences in the number and variety of vocational choices, preferences and aspirations, *Journal of Occupational Psychology*, 51, 119-125
Hughes, E.C. (1958) The study of occupations, In R.K. Merton, L. Broomand and L. Cotrell (Eds.), *Sociology Today*, Basic Books, New York
Hunt, A. (1968) *A Survey of Women's Employment*,

H.M.S.O., London
Hunt, A. (1975) Management Attitudes and Practices Towards Women at Work, Department of Employment, Office of Population Censuses and Surveys, SS021, H.M.S.O., London
Ireson, C. (1978) In Stromberg, A.H. and Harkness,S., (Eds.), Women Working: Theories and Facts in Perspective, Mayfield, California
Jackson, R. (1973) Careers Guidance, Practice and Problems, Edward Arnold, Maidenhead
Jahoda, G. (1952) Job attitudes and job choice among Secondary Modern School leavers, Parts 1 and 2, Occupational Psychology, 26, 125-140 and 206-224
Jahoda, G. and Chalmers, A. (1963) The youth employment service: A consumer perspective, Occupational Psychology, 37, 1, 20-43
Jencks, C., Smith, M., Acland, H., Bane, M.J., Cohen, D., Gintis, H., Heyns, B. and Michelson, S. (1975) Inequality: A Reassessment of the Effect of Family and Schooling in America, Peregrine, London
Jordan, D. (1941) The attitudes of central school pupils to certain school subjects and the correlation between attitudes and attainment, British Journal of Educational Psychology, 11, 21-44
Kahn, R.L. and Katz, D. (1960) Leadership practices in relation to productivity and morale, In Cartwright, D. and Zander, A. (Eds), Group Dynamics: Research and Theory. Vol. 2, Harper and Row, New York
Keil, E.T. (1977) Becoming a Worker, Leicestershire Committee for Education and Industry and the Training Services Agency, Leicester
King, R. (1969) Values and Involvement in a Grammar School, Routledge and Kegan Paul, London
Kopp, C.B. (1979) Becoming Female: Perspectives on Development, Plenum Press, New York
Lacey, C. (1970) Hightown Grammar: The School as a Social System, Manchester University Press, Manchester
Lacey, C. (1974) Destreaming in a pressured academic environment. In Eggleston, J. (Ed.), Contemporary Research in the Sociology of Education, Methuen, London
Lavin, D. (1965) Prediction of Academic Performance, John Wiley and Sons, New York
Lawler, E.E., Kuleck, W.J., Rhode, J.G. and Sorensen, J.E. (1975) Job choice and post

decision dissonance, *Organizational Behaviour and Human Performance*, 13, 133-145

Locksley, A. and Douvan, E. (1978) Problem behaviour in adolescents, In Gomberg, E. and Frank, V. (Eds), *Sex Differences in Disturbed Behaviour*, Bruner Mazel, New York

Mack, J. (1977) From school to work, *New Society*, 10th March, 489-491

Maizels, J. (1970) *Adolescents Needs and the Transition from school to Work*, Athlone Press, London

Maslow, A.H. (1954) *Motivation and Personality*, Harper, New York

McGauvran, M.E. (1955) A study of the relationship between attitudes towards school and scholastic success at the high school and college level, Unpublished PhD thesis, Boston University School of Education

Mednick, M.T.S., Tangri, S.S. and Hoffman, L.W. (1975) *Women and Achievement: Social and Motivational Analyses*, Wiley, London

Meyer, W.J. and Thompson, G.C. (1956) Sex differences in the distribution of teacher approval and disapproval, *Journal of Education Psychology*, 47, 385- 396

Michael, W.B., Herrold, E.E. and Cryan, E.W. (1951) Survey of student-teacher relationships, *Journal of Educational Research*, 44, 657-674

Miller, D.C. and Form, W.H. (1964) *Industrial Sociology*, Harper and Row, New York

Moor, C.H. (1976) *From School to Work: Effective Counselling and Guidance*, Sage Publications, London

Parsons, F. (1909) *Choosing a Vocation*, Houghton Mifflin, Boston

Passow, A.H., Goldberg, M. and Tannembaum, A.J.(Eds) (1967) *Education of the Disadvantaged*, Holt, Rinehart and Winston, New York

Paul, L. (1979) Sixteen year olds' images of work, *Personnel Review*, 8, 1, 10-13

Pettman, B.O. (1979) Women in work, and equal opportunities audit, *Employee Relations*, 1, 1, 19-23

Postlethwaite, K. and Denton, C. (1978) *Streams for the future? The long term effects of early streaming and non-streaming - the final report of the Banbury Enquiry*, Pubansco, Banbury

Pumfrey, P.D. and Warm, H. (1972) Vocational maturity, educational visits and the IVth form leaver, *Careers Bulletin*, Spring, 20-25

Rauta, I. and Hunt, A. (1975) Fifth Form Girls: Their Hopes for the Future, H.M.S.O., London

Reiss, A.J. (1961) Occupational and Social Status, The Free Press of Glencoe, New York

Richardson, M.S. (1978) Vocational Development, In Jersild, A.T., Brook, J.S. and Brook, D.W.(Eds) The Psychology of Adolescence, Collier Macmillan, London

Riesman, D. (1950) The Lonely Crowd, Oxford University Press, Oxford

Riesman, D. (1952) Faces in the Crowd, Oxford University Press, Oxford

Roberts, K. (1968) The organization of education and the ambitions of school-leavers: A Comparative review, Comparative Education, 4, 87-96

Roberts, K. (1970) The Youth Employment Service, the schools and preparation of school leavers for employment, Vocational Aspects of Education, 22, 52, 81-89

Roberts, K. (1975) The Developmental Theory of Occupational Choice: A Critique and an Alternative, In G. Esland et al. (Eds) People and Work, Holmes McDougall, Edinburgh

Roberts, K. (1976) Where is the careers service heading? Careers Bulletin, Spring, 26-30

Roberts, K. (1977), The social conditions, consequences and limitations of careers guidance, British Journal of Guidance and Counselling, 5, 1, 1-9

Rodger, A. (1961) Arranging jobs for the young, New Society, 10

Row, A. and Siegelman, M. (1964) The Origin of Interests, American Personnel and Guidance Association, Washington

Rutter, M. (1976) Helping Troubled Children, Penguin, Harmondsworth

Rutter, M., Maugham, B., Mortimore, P. and Ouston,J. (1979) Fifteen Thousand Hours: Secondary Schools and their effects on Children, Open Books, London

Schein, E.H. (1964) The mechanisms of change, In Bennis, W.G., Schein, E.H., Steel, W. and Berlow, D.C. (Eds) Interpersonal Dynamics, The Dorsey Press, Homewood, Illinois

Schlossberg, N. and Pietrofesa, J. (1973) Perspectives on Counselling Bias: Implications for counsellor education, Counselling Psychologist, 4, 44-54

Serbin, L.A., O'Leary, K.D., Kent, R.N. and Tonick, I.J. (1973) A comparison of teacher response to the preacademic and problem behaviour of boys

213

and girls, Child Development, 44, 796-804
Shaw, J. (1976) Finishing School: Some Implications of Sex-Segregated Education, In Barker, D.L. and Allen, S. (Eds) Sexual Divisions and Society: Process and Change, Tavistock, London
Shaw, M. and McCuen, J. (1960) The onset of academic underachievement in bright children, Journal of Educational Psychology, 51, 103-108
Shinn, E.O. (1956) Interest and intelligence as related to achievement in tenth grade, California Journal of Educational Research, 7, 217-220
Srole, L. (1956a) Social integration and certain corollaries: An exploratory study, American Sociological Review, December, 709-716
Srole, L. (1956b) Anomie, authoritarianism and prejudice, American Journal of Sociology, 62 63-67
Sternglanz, S. and Serbin, L. (1974) Sex role sterotyping in children's television programs, Developmental Psychology, 10, 710- 715
Super, D.E. (1957) The Psychology of Careers, Harper and Row, New York
Super, D.E. and Overstreet, P.L. (1968) The Vocational Maturity of Ninth Grade Boys, Teachers College, New York
Super, D.E., Starishevslky, R., Matlin, N. and Jordan, J.P. (1963) Career Development: Self Concept Theory, College Entrance Examination Board, Princeton
Swift, B. (1973) Job orientations and the transition from school to work: A longitudinal study, British Journal of Guidance and Counselling, 1, 1, 62-78
Taylor, P.H. (1962) Children's evaluations of the characteristics of a good teacher, British Journal of Educational Psychology, 32, 258-266
Thibaut, J.W. and Kelley, H.H. (1959) The Social Psychology of Groups, Wiley, New York
Van Maanen, J. (1976) Breaking in: Socialization to Work, In Dubin, R. (Ed.), Handbook of Work, Organization and Society, Rand McNally, Chicago
Veness, T. (1962) School Leavers - Their Aspirations and Expectations, Methuen, London
Vroom, V.H. (1964) Work and Motivation, Wiley, New York
Vroom, V.H. and Deci, E.L. (1971) The stability of post-decisional dissonance: a follow-up study on the job attitudes of business school graduates, Organizational Behaviour and Human

Performance, 6, 36-49

Wallis, D. (1978) Some pressing problems for research in vocational guidance, Journal of Occupational Psychology, 51, 7-18

Wanous, J.P. (1975) Effects of realistic job previews on job acceptance, job attitudes and job survival, Journal of Applied Psychology, 58, 327-332

Wanous, J.P. (1977) Organizational Entry: Newcomers moving from outside to inside, Psychological Bulletin, 84, 4, 601-618

Warr, P. and Wall, T. (1975) Work and Well Being, Penguin, Harmondsworth

Watts, A.G. and Kidd, J.M. (1978) Evaluating the effectiveness of careers guidance: A review of the British research, Journal of Occupational Psychology, 51, 3, 235-248

Weitz, J. (1957) Job expectancy and survival, Journal of Applied Psychology, 40, 346-361

Wilkins, L.T. (1955) The Adolescent in Britain, The Social Survey, H.M.S.O., London

Williams, J.A. (1979) Psychological Androgeny and Mental Health, In Fuller, M. and Boden, G. (Eds) Sex-Role Stereotyping, Tavistock, London

Willis, P.E. (1978) Learning to Labour, Saxon House, London

Wilson, C. (1979) The Development of Self, In Coleman, J.C. (Ed.) The School Years: Current Issues in the Socialization of Young People, Methuen, London

Wilson, M.D. (1953) The vocational preferences of secondary modern schoolchildren, British Journal of Educational Psychology, 23, 97-113 and 163-179

Youthaid (1979) Study of the Transition from School to Working Life, Youthaid, London

INDEX

Academic achievement 12, 13, 21, 39, 40, 178
academic values in school 14, 37, 39, 132, 174
adolescence 39-41, 109, 160, 173, 176-181, 187-188
alienation 38, 164-167, 172, 181, 188
Allen, E.A. 22, 39
applying for jobs 56, 57-76
Arvidson, G.L. 21, 28
Ashton, D. 9, 61, 88
attitudes 13, 14, 15, 20, 41, 100; to the careers service 20; to co-workers 10, 19, 135, 136; of parents 32; to school 10, 11, 13, 14, 21-41, 159; to supervisors 10, 11, 15, 19, 22-23, 134-143, 173; to society 19, 160, 164-167; of teachers 14, 21, 177; to teachers 11, 19, 21-41, 135-143, 159, 173, 174, 176, 177; to training 99-100; to work 10, 11, 15, 19, 23, 114-133, 178, 182

banding 12, 16, 17, 19, 159, 166-167, 172, 174-176, 182, 184; and aims and attainments 80, 82-84, 92; and attitudes to supervisors 135, 138; and attitudes to teachers and schools 26-28, 32, 37-38, 114; and attitudes to training 100-102; and attitudes to work 114, 125-126, 127, 132; and entry to work 102; and job changing 153; and occupational choice 44, 46, 49-50, 55-56
Barker Lunn, J. 12, 13, 14, 21, 28
Baxter, J.L. 144
Bower, T.G.R. 173
Bray, D.W. 98
Brown, G.W. 160, 166
Buehler, C. 4
Burns, R.B. 188
Bush, R.N. 22

Campbell, P. 177
careers 3-5, 8, 42, 44, 53, 96, 181-189; advisory service 20, 55, 57-58, 65-70, 75-76, 179, 181-189; guidance 7-11, 17-18, 42, 49, 55, 66-76, 86, 91-93, 96, 147, 181-189; interview 19, 66-70; teachers 1-6, 17, 49, 55, 71-73, 86, 115, 157, 181-189, teaching

216

11, 17-18, 20, 46-49,
  56, 58, 71-73, 74-75,
  86-87, 92, 93, 112,
  114, 127, 132, 147, 157,
  169, 181-189
Carter, M. 10, 55, 59, 62,
  63, 64, 66, 77, 78, 95-
  97, 107, 108, 110, 144,
  146-147, 158
Cherry, N. 9, 144-145
Child, D. 4-6
Clarke, A.M. 7
Coleman, J.C. 109, 188
Coleman, J.S. 178
comparison levels 147- 152
conditions of work 8, 19,
  89-91, 120-133, 147,
  151, 157, 178, 183, 184
co-workers 9, 10, 19, 96,
  97, 100, 102, 122, 135,
  136, 138, 139, 141, 155
Crites, J.O. 42
Crowther report, 11, 85
curricula 71, 99, 189

Daws, P. 9
De Fleur, M.L. 112
De Groat, A.F. 39, 40
D.E.S. 189
developmental theories of
  occupational choice 2-7,
  8, 12, 43-44, 46, 49,
  50, 53, 55, 56, 77, 86,
  91, 92, 181-189
developmental approach to
  careers guidance 12, 18,
  46, 49, 86, 92, 127,
  181-189
differentialist approach
  to careers guidance 12,
  43, 46, 53, 55, 56, 77,
  86, 92-93, 127, 146,
  181-189
Dominick, J.R. 179
Douvan, E. 23, 39, 179,
  180

education 8, 14, 69-70,
  77, 85, 99, 100, 102,
  104, 184; and ability
  12-15, 28, 37, 46, 50,
  61, 85, 100, 175, 185;
  and attainment 14;
  institutions 8; and
  qualifications 8, 85
Emmett, W. 177
employers 9, 11, 20, 55,
  57, 69, 95, 103, 105,
  115, 134, 145, 154,
  155
entry into work 15, 19,
  91, 94-113, 149, 188
Equal Opportunities
  Commission 105
examinations 13, 16-17,
  28, 37, 61, 71, 82,
  89, 139, 146; CSEs 17,
  23, 28, 51, 80, 175;
  GCEs 16, 23, 28, 51,
  80, 175; passes 19,
  28, 38, 51, 61, 62,
  64, 82, 100, 166, 172,
  145, 184
expectations of the
  future 159-164, 180;
  of the world of work
  106-108, 115, 119-120,
  121, 125, 132, 150,
  176, 178; and help in
  finding jobs 66-68,
  73-75, 86; and job
  choice 52-55, 57, 179

Ferri, E. 13, 39
Field, D. 9
Finlayson, D.J. 38
Friedersdorf, N. 177

Ginzberg, E. 2-4, 7, 44,
  46, 86, 145, 155, 181
Gove, W.R. 15, 166
Gray, H.L. 110

Handyside, J.D. 22, 135
Hargreaves, D.H. 14, 21,
  37, 61, 174
Havighurst, R.J. 4
Hayes, J. 7, 74, 110,
  122, 150, 157, 186
help, sources of 57-76
Hill, J.M.M. 110, 150
Holland, J.L. 6, 43

217

Homans, G.C. 147
home-life 19, 160-161
hopes for the future 15, 19, 42, 98
Hopson, B. 7
Hoult, P.P. 45
Hours of work 98, 127-128, 150, 178
Hughes, E.C. 110
Hunt, A. 15, 117, 129, 162

identity 42, 164, 166
induction to work organization 96-100, 105-106, 112, 117
influence 64, 73
intelligence 6, 39, 72, 178
Ireson, C. 40, 177, 179

Jackson, R. 7
Jahoda, G. 55, 66, 110, 150
Jencks, C. 12, 13
job aims 10, 11, 76, 77-93
job applications 57-76, 150
job attainments 10, 11
job changing 9-11, 20, 69-70, 95, 119, 128-132, 144-158
jobs held 20
job interest 121-125, 129
job interviews 20
jobs, methods of finding 10, 18-19, 57-76
job opportunities 51, 53; local 8, 9, 18, 43, 49, 69, 77, 86, 87, 186
job prospects 3
job satisfaction 43, 57, 69, 115, 117-119, 126, 129, 132, 148, 150
job security 3
job stability 128-129
Jordan, D. 21, 28

Kahn, R.L. 134

Keil, E.T. 97
Kidd, J. 9
King, R. 174
Kopp, C.B. 15

Lacey, C. 12
Lavin, D. 177
life-changes 160-161, 180
Locksley, 180

Mack, J. 110, 150
Maizels, J. 11, 22, 23, 24, 29, 41, 52, 54, 58, 62, 63, 66, 78, 79, 88, 96-97, 110, 124, 126, 127, 135, 138, 144, 149, 150, 162
management 95, 97, 98, 129
Maslow, A.H. 7
matching 43, 46, 55, 146; process 6, 50
McGauvran, M.E. 21, 28
media 1, 53, 110, 150, 179
Mednick, M.T.S. 105
metamorphosis 110-112
Meyer, W.J. 40
Michael, W.B. 22
Miller, D.C. 145, 155
mining 16, 45, 54, 72-74, 80, 81, 92, 102, 148, 168
mixed ability teaching 12-15, 17, 85
Moor, C.H. 110, 150

National Institute of Industrial Psychology 135

occupational aims 77-93
occupational attainments 45, 77-93, 124
occupational choice 12, 42-56, 73, 77, 78, 91, 146; important factors in 168-169; theories of 2-11, 43-44, 50-51, 53, 55, 56, 69-70, 77,

78, 92, 146, 181-189
opportunity structure 8, 18, 44, 181
Overstreet, P.L. 6
overtime 127, 178

parents 1, 14, 32, 73-74, 79, 90, 110, 177
parent-child relationship 7, 19, 43, 55, 161, 166, 172
Parsons, F. 43
Passow, A. 12
Paul, L. 97
pay (and wages) 3, 19, 71, 89, 91, 93, 98, 107, 126-128, 129, 131, 132, 148, 150-151, 128, 157, 176, 178, 186
personality 5, 6, 7, 43, 70, 146, 152, 155
Pettman, B.O. 103
policy 12
Postlethwaite, K. 13
promotion 126-127, 128-129, 132, 162, 168, 176
Pumfrey P.D. 74, 158, 186

Rauta, I. 168
realistic job previews 99, 113, 150; reasons for accepting jobs 88-93; for job changes 155-158; for job choices 44, 45, 47, 52-56
Reiss, A.J. 45
research methods 2, 16, 86, 95, 115-116, 151
Richardson, M.S. 42
Riesman, D. 52, 54
Roberts, K. 4, 7-9, 44, 50, 53, 77, 86, 87, 92, 110, 150, 158, 181-187
Rodger, A. 145
Roe, A. 7, 43
Rutter, M. 7, 38, 134, 142, 174-175

Schein, E.H. 110

Schlossberg, N. 177
school 8, 11, 63, 77, 99, 103, 124, 139, 140, 141, 149, 159 169; and academic organization 12-15, 21-22, 26, 28, 37-38, 41, 49, 51, 84, 86, 132, 142, 166-167, 173-176, 182; attitudes to 10, 11, 13, 14, 19, 21-41, 159; comprehensive 17, 31, 32, 41, 175; ethos 37, 114, 142, 173-176; grammar 8, 12, 16, 31, 41, 44, 175; help in finding jobs 57-76; junior and primary 13-14, 21, 28, 40; leaving 11, 30, 34; liking 29-34; secondary modern 8, 17, 31, 175; social institution 12-15, 21-22, 28, 38, 40-41, 132, 142, 173-176
self, actualisation 8, 86, 183; awareness 18, 43, 46, 55, 69, 145, 184, 186; concept 5, 6, 8, 39, 43, 46, 91, 132, 178, 183, 188; confidence 18; esteem 117, 188; image 14, 15, 39
Serbin, L.A. 39
sex differences, in alienation 165-166; in attitudes to leaving school 34, 38-41; in attitudes to school 31-33, 35, 40-41; in attitudes to teachers 23, 29-30, 35, 38-41; in attitudes to work 116-120; in changes in home life 160-162; in conditions of work 120, 125, 129; in expectations of the future 162-164; in hours and

219

pay 127-128, 130; in important factors in job choices 168-169; in introductions to work 105-106; in job changing 153, 157; in job interest 121-122, 123, 125; in promotion 128-129, 131; in training received 101, 103, 105; in the transition 15-16, 20, 23, 34-36; 171-172, 176-181; in work experience 74
sex discrimination 15, 103-105, 117, 129, 179, 187, 188; sex roles 19, 160-169, 172, 176-181
sex role socialization 23, 39, 176-181
sex role stereotyping 167-168, 172, 176-181
Shaw, J. 39
Shaw, M. 177
Shinn, E.O. 21, 28
Siegelmann, M. 7
sixth form 16, 17, 208
social aspects of work 122, 126-127
social exchange theory 147-155
socialization 8, 15, 23, 39, 44, 95, 96, 98, 109, 110-113, 188; to occupations 94-113; to organizations 94-113; to work 109-113, 119, 134, 139, 141
socio-economic background 5, 7, 12-15, 29, 31, 32, 34, 37, 50, 56, 79
socio-economic status of jobs 45, 46, 48, 50, 51, 61, 62, 63, 79, 80-86, 92, 126, 142, 153, 166, 172, 182
sources of help in finding jobs 57-76, 78
Srole, L. 164-167
statistical testing 10, 78
status 42, 45, 48-51, 120, 126-127, 139, 149, 166, 174, 180
Sternglanz, S. 179
streaming 12-14,17, 21, 23, 28, 37-38, 79, 100, 174, 175
sub cultures 13, 14, 37, 100, 167
Super, D. 4-6, 18, 43, 86, 145, 181, 187
supervisors 10, 11, 15, 19, 22-23, 97, 134-143, 155, 173, 174, 176
Swift, B. 14

Taylor, P.H. 22
teachers 16, 19, 20, 21-24, 78, 135-141, 174, 177; attitudes of 17, 21-41, 176; attitudes to 11, 21-41, 139, 140, 158, 173, 174-176, 177, 178; stereotypes of 21; relationships with 22, 23, 24, 37, 38-41
Thibaut, J.W. 148-149
trade unions 95
training 19, 90, 91, 94, 97, 98, 99-105, 108, 112-113, 120 127, 176, 178, 188
Training Opportunities Schemes 105, 108
unemployment 59, 63, 78, 84, 89, 92, 146, 148, 152, 182-183, 187

Van Maanen, J. 110-112
Veness, T. 11, 52-54, 78, 162
vocational aspirations 39, 45
vocational choice 6, 43, 145
vocational guidance 9, 11, 17-19
Vroom, V.H. 45, 110, 98

Wages 3, 19, 71, 89, 91,
   93, 98, 107, 126-128,
   129, 131, 132, 148, 150-
   151, 157, 176, 178, 186
Wallis, D. 45
Wanous, J.P. 98, 150, 186
Warr, P.B. 185
Watts, A. 9, 69, 185
Weitz, J. 99, 186
Wilkins, L.T. 162
Williams, J. 166
Willis, P. 37, 38, 174
Wilson, M.D. 110, 150
work experience 17, 66, 71,
   74, 75, 98-99, 113, 150,
   171, 172, 188
work organizations 22, 53,
   74, 98, 99, 102, 109,
   110, 114, 115

Youthaid 99, 186
Youth Employment Service 10
Youth Opportunities
   Programme 108